WHEN
COUPLES
PRAY
TOGETHER

WHEN COUPLES PRAY TOGETHER

*Creating Intimacy and
Spiritual Wholeness*

*Jan Stoop
and
David Stoop*

SERVANT PUBLICATIONS
ANN ARBOR, MICHIGAN

Vine Books is an imprint of Servant Publications especially designed to serve evangelical Christians.

Published in association with the literary agency of Alive Communications, Inc., 1465 Kelly Johnson Blvd., Suite 320, Colorado Springs, CO 80920.

To protect the privacy of some of the individuals whose stories are told in this book, names and characterizations have been fictionalized, although they are based on real events. With permission, real names and events are portrayed in most of the stories.

Published by Servant Publications
P.O. Box 8617
Ann Arbor, Michigan 48107

Cover design: Left Coast Design, Portland, Oregon
Cover photo: © John Feingersh/The Stock Market. Used by permission.

00 01 02 03 10 9 8 7 6 5 4 3 2 1

Printed in the United States of America
ISBN 1-56955-108-1

Cataloging-in-Publication Data on file at the Library of Congress.

Dedicated to
all the praying couples who helped us
make this book a reality

~

CONTENTS

PREFACE

There has never been a topic about which we have been more enthusiastic than the subject of how couples can develop spiritual intimacy through praying together. But when it came to sitting down and writing about it, we found that it was a topic that brought us to a great sense of inadequacy, even though we have been praying together daily for almost thirty years.

We do not in any way hold ourselves up as experts on prayer, nor have we tried to make this an exhaustive study on prayer. Many others have already done that, excellently. Yet, with a sense of awe, and a bit of hesitancy, we want to share our own struggle with making praying together a priority in our marriage. We hope that our story, as well as the others we have included, will challenge and motivate you to put praying together first and allow God to do as he will in the process.

We've found over the years that as we have prayed together regularly, it has helped us to put other things in our marriage in order. Something about that daily time of accountability before the Lord has created an openness in us about other aspects of our relationship. This has become a part of our communication not only with God, but also with each other. God has met us dramatically in that process and has done some exciting things when we've stepped out of his way and sought to learn more about his perspective and sovereignty.

So much of the effort it takes to sustain a marriage relationship involves the working out of issues and conflicts that require us to face each other. Yet, there is another stance couples can take. Instead of facing each other, trying desperately to work out our problems on our own, we can stand together, holding hands, facing forward, looking together to the future and to what God has planned for us as a couple. One couple who took our challenge wrote, "Our praying together certainly brought us closer spiritually. We have a different viewpoint and attitude when we are standing together before our Father." This is the extraordinary couple God is looking for—two people who are watching with expectancy to see what God has in store for them.

This doesn't mean there aren't still times when we must turn and face each other to deal with issues and conflicts. What it does mean is that there is an added emphasis—that of finding together our voice as a couple, inviting God to do something extraordinary in our relationship and in our world. A couple who acknowledges that God is inviting them to join him in what he is already doing in their world is an awesome thing! And praying together is the beginning point. We challenge you to start today and see what God will do in your marriage!

We wanted this to be an encouraging book—one that would challenge you to try something new, not just make you feel guilty for not doing it. We also wanted to write something that would not only motivate you, but also provide some practical ways to help you actually get started. Whether you are newly married or celebrating sixty years of marriage, it's never too late to begin. If you as a couple are already praying together, we hope you will find enjoyment and affirmation of the journey you've already begun.

We believe that to dissect prayer or to analyze it too deeply is to destroy its personal nature, so we rely mostly on stories of our own experiences, or those of others who have undertaken the same journey. We hope the stories will portray real people with whom you can identify.

We know that individual prayer is a spiritual discipline. As with any discipline in life, we never arrive at a place where it doesn't take effort. A daily commitment to follow through is required. As we practice a discipline, we find it is something we can always learn more about. Praying together is also a discipline, though here it takes two willing hearts. But since it is a discipline, praying together is something that we never fully master—we will always be students. It is our prayer that this book will become a textbook you use as a couple as you meet with the God of the universe together in the school of prayer. Will you join us in the journey?

ACKNOWLEGMENTS

We were overwhelmed by the responses of so many couples who have expressed an interest in praying together. We want to thank them for jumping in, stepping off the curb, and making the commitment to pray together for a six-week period. We honor you! A special thank-you to those of you who took the time and energy to fill out our questionnaire and give us your stories about what happened when you prayed together. And to those couples who have already been praying together and volunteered their stories about what has happened when they prayed, we give God praise for you. You know what it's like to be in the trenches through the hard times, and you have made it through! How awesome it is to hear from couples like you who offer hope and encouragement to those couples who are having a hard time making prayer a priority in their marriages. We know that God is at work in you. You challenged us too!

When Bert Ghezzi from Servant Publications said, "Would you be interested in doing a book on couples and prayer?" we both looked at each other and said, "Would we ever!" We both thought, *he's asking the right couple and he doesn't even know that we have had a passion in the past few years to help other couples develop spiritual intimacy in their marriages by praying together.* Thank you, Bert, for asking!

We did not even consider how difficult it might have been

to work with an editor who did not understand what we were trying to say in this book about couples and prayer. We did not even think to ask God about that! But in his wisdom he knew just who we needed even when we did not ask. He gave us Kathy Deering. Kathy and her husband Mike have been praying together for all the years of their marriage. As we got to know Kathy over the telephone, one day she quietly told us that she understood our challenge because she and Mike had made that commitment years ago! We could hardly believe it—an editor who had experienced exactly what we were talking about and one who would even contribute her story. (You will read about Kathy and Mike in chapter seven.) We know beyond a shadow of a doubt that this was all part of the plan. For God is looking for couples who are willing to give over a part of the time he has allotted them together so that they can develop a deeper relationship with him. Kathy, you understood this. Thank you!

A discipline for the spiritual life is, when the dust of history is blown away, nothing but an activity undertaken to bring us into more effective cooperation with Christ and his Kingdom. When we understand that grace (charis) is a gift (charisma), we then see that to grow in grace is to grow in what is given to us of God and by God. The disciplines are then, in the clearest sense, a means to that grace and also to those gifts. Spiritual disciplines, "exercises unto godliness," are only activities undertaken to make us capable of receiving more of his life and power without harm to ourselves or others.[1]

Dallas Willard

Part One

WHY PRAY TOGETHER?

Chapter One

YEARNING AND HIDING

So make every effort to apply the benefits of these promises to your life. Then your faith will produce a life of moral excellence. A life of moral excellence leads to knowing God better. Knowing God leads to self-control. Self-control leads to patient endurance, and patient endurance leads to godliness. Godliness leads to love for other Christians, and finally you will grow to have genuine love for everyone.

2 PETER 1:5-7, NLT

It was chilly and crisp—a perfect day for driving. We had just finished leading a couples' retreat in New York and had decided that we would take a couple of days to drive up into Vermont to one of our favorite parts of the country. We were looking forward to seeing the beautiful colors of the leaves that grace the New England landscape during October. But somehow this particular year the winds had stripped the leaves early and the trees looked forlorn and bare. After a day and a half of driving, we decided to head back to New York instead and go see the college campus where we had spent our first two years of marriage.

We hadn't been there for many years. What memories flooded over us as we toured the campus and looked at the beautiful views from the dorms and library that we had taken so for granted many years earlier. We drove the narrow, curvy, hillside streets around the town of Nyack, and looked for the house in which we had had our first apartment. Finally, there it was on that tiny street, looking so much smaller than we had remembered. We were overcome with flashbacks.

The little old lady who had owned the house many years ago was so gracious in letting students stay there, but she also expected a lot from them, especially appreciation for her handiwork. She had painted our little apartment in her own special way with the ceiling blue, like the sky, she explained, and the walls green, so that we could experience it like the outdoors, she proudly said. And there was another catch. She informed us that if we wanted to take this lovely apartment she would need daily access to our apartment to use our refrigerator, as she did not have one of her own. (She added that sometimes in the winter, she put her things out on the porch to keep them cold, and wouldn't bother us as much then.) What interesting and disturbing times we had those first few months of our marriage, living with Mrs. Tallman, struggling to set limits on her intrusions into our new and shaky relationship!

We sat in the car and talked about some of the very hard times we had experienced trying to adjust to each other. We had yearned for a peaceful settled relationship, but neither of us had any idea how to move toward it. We fought and threatened, we loved and cared, but we did not even think about the dimension of spiritual intimacy, which might have made the difference in how we related to each other.

We had both accepted Jesus into our lives as Lord and

Savior; Jan as a young child and Dave as a teenager, but we had no idea about how that personal relationship with God could add the depth of spiritual intimacy to our relationship. We went to a Christian college, sat in numerous meetings, prayed individually and at meals, studied the Bible and took classes on the Bible, and listened to our favorite Christian speakers on tape. But back then, none of these made our individual relationships with God into a *shared* journey. Spiritual intimacy was something that we both wanted but did not talk about until much later in our marriage.

JAN: Our story about praying together begins with me because, in looking back, I believe I was such a big part of the problem. You see, from the human standpoint, I was probably a setup for failure from the beginning—at least in the area of developing spiritual intimacy with my husband. I think I hit the ground running when I entered this world. My personality is such that it keeps me wanting more and more out of life. I try hard at everything I do. Add to that my perfectionistic tendencies and you can see the setup.

I don't know about you, but I always thought that if you worked hard enough at something, there would be results. That sounds right, doesn't it? I also believed that something could always be done about anything. After all, that was what my father believed, and he instilled that attitude in me. So when it came to the subject of praying together with my husband, I figured I'd approach that area just as I had approached almost everything else in my life—with enthusiasm. My enthusiasm was also fed by the fact that I came from a family where we prayed out loud together every night, on our knees. Why should I expect that the family my husband and I were creating would be any different? I also knew my mom and dad prayed together regularly. I can remember coming in late in the evening as a teenager and seeing my mom and dad on their knees together in the living room.

Prayer was important to me, even as a little girl. It was something I did individually, and it was something I really enjoyed in our family. So it was only natural that when I got married, I had expectations about how we would pray together. What I painfully found out was that the man I had married not only had a very different personality from mine, but he came from a very different family and did not have the experience of praying together as a family on a daily basis. It didn't take too long to realize that he also had very different ideas about our life together, and that he certainly was not going to simply follow my agenda, regardless of how spiritual it was.

It wasn't easy to come crashing up against these major differences between Dave and myself. Even our styles of communication were different. For example, one difference is that I like to sit down and talk about things. I prefer to have people interact with me face-to-face without any distractions such as television or newspapers. I mistakenly thought everyone felt that way, but Dave didn't. He needs time to work things out in his head. But to me, it seems reasonable that when you say something to someone, there ought to be some response. I prefer a verbal response, but with Dave I was eventually willing to accept even a nod or some other acknowledgment of what I was saying. Dave has often told me that if I had just waited a little longer, I would have gotten a response. But I often gave up long before the response ever came. Instead, I tried harder to get him to talk. And the harder I tried, the more resistance I felt from him.

Now, if we were talking about spiritual things, especially about praying together (and I know I brought it up often), it seemed the resistance became even stronger. Whenever I brought up the subject, Dave would become silent. Or he would gradually change the subject. Or if I caught him in a particularly talkative mood, he would simply say, "I'll think about it." For years, my own heart hungered for the spiritual intimacy I had always wanted in my marriage, but Dave's consistent response seemed to be, "Not yet"—typical, I know now, of his "wait and see" attitude, and his need to process things before responding.

In Dave's defense, it wasn't that he was not interested in spiritual things. In fact, during those early years of our marriage, Dave was leading an independent youth ministry, and then served on the pastoral staff of several churches. It wasn't that he never prayed. In fact, he could pray with other people in his office at the church. He could pray in front of a Sunday school class, or even from the pulpit in church. He would pray with our children and our family at times, and he would even pray with my family when we were visiting them. I know he prayed on his own as well. It was just that he would never pray with me.

When I asked him about how his family handled prayer, he said that his only memories of his family praying together were at meals. If his parents ever prayed together, he didn't know about it. He would often say, "I guess I'm just not a prayer warrior like you."

Well, that didn't feel very good. In reality, I was struggling with my own time for prayer as I juggled caring for three children, trying to work part-time, and being part of the youth ministry that Dave was heading up. All along, I hoped that Dave would rescue me and take the burden of this issue from me by "taking charge." I wanted him to take the initiative to put that spiritual aspect in place in our relationship. Wasn't being a spiritual leader part of his job as a husband? I thought so, especially as I continued to take what seemed to me to be all the responsibility for caring about the things I felt should at least be shared between us.

How I struggled with my expectations! Our early years of marriage were difficult as we tried to relate to each other—many times we thought we would not make it. The wonderful spiritual aspect of marriage I had envisioned seemed impossible as our relationship slowly gave way to the day-by-day survival mode. I found I was powerless to change much of anything.

Here's where my perfectionism only added to the problem. I continually wanted more out of our relationship, but I had no idea how to go about getting it. I remained stuck in the same old pattern—feeling that if I just tried a little harder, the problem would resolve itself. I remember once, in a sharing time with other pastors' wives, how we all laughed as we discovered how many of us had used the same tactics to encourage our husbands to be more involved with us in the spiritual aspects of our marriages. I was amazed at how many of us had left the Bible open on our husband's plate at a holiday dinner as a not-so-subtle clue that he was to take charge and read it aloud to the family. I know I did that more often than I care to admit.

Over time, I moved from more overt clues to trying more subtly (or so I thought) to get Dave to think that it was at least partly his idea, hoping that then he would cooperate. We laugh together now at some of the outrageous things I did to try to encourage his participation. I remember planning carefully how I would drop little hints as to what he was to do. He never picked up on them.

All this time, I was trying so hard to get Dave to take the lead, as I felt a husband should, that I was negating my own responsibility for taking the steps necessary to get my spiritual life in order. Yes, I was praying on my own during that time. I also prayed with the kids and for them. I went into their rooms and prayed with them as they went to sleep, and I went back into their rooms and prayed for them as they slept. When they were tiny, I prayed for them as I rocked them and prayed for the mate that they would someday marry. What wonderful times those were—but I wanted so much to share it with Dave. Sometimes I think I wanted spiritual intimacy so much that I allowed my obsession with it to overshadow the goodness of what we did experience together. Worst of all, I often forgot to pray about the very thing that was bothering me!

Recently, in a workshop we were conducting on this subject, someone shared with us the statistic that only 4 percent of Christian couples actually pray together on a regular basis. There were several hundred people in the audience, and no one refuted the statistic. Maybe this was because only 4 percent of those attending actually prayed together on a regular basis. If I had known that statistic some years earlier, I might have better understood our struggle and not felt alone as I tried so hard to "fix it."

What we've also found out, in talking with many pastors and their wives, is that couples in the ministry probably don't pray together any more often than do those in their congregations. That 4 percent statistic may apply to them as well. What was so frustrating for us in those early years was, and unfortunately still is, an all-too-common problem for Christian couples: how to overcome the personal resistances, the personalities, the family backgrounds, the expectations, the marriage problems—all barriers thrown in our paths by the evil one, who desperately wants to prevent couples from praying together!

Perhaps you're wondering what was going through Dave's mind during those early years. Let's find out.

DAVE: Jan remembers it all very well. I was very aware of her desire for us to pray together but never could convince myself that the effort was worth the risk. What risk, you might be thinking? Well, it seemed like a big risk to me.

To begin with, I didn't have any good memories of my family praying together, like Jan did. The few times I remember my parents trying to hold family devotions, I was a restless teenager and couldn't wait for it to be over. I think my restlessness and my resistance was too much for my parents, as they tried only a couple of times before it was forgotten. I had had no example of the meaningfulness of praying together as a family.

I remember going to prayer meetings at church every Wednesday night, and those were not good memories either. Those meetings seemed like they were very long, lonely, and boring. There never were very many people there, and everything had to have this "holy hush" about it. When I got old enough to go to the youth group for prayer meeting, it didn't get any better for me. What I remember most is how my knees ached, as I had to kneel on the hard floor. As I got older, I was expected to pray in the group, and I remember rehearsing what I was going to pray. The intimacy Jan had experienced in her family as they prayed together was never a part of my experience, either at home or at church.

So part of my reluctance was quite simply, "What's the big deal about praying together?" Just as long as I prayed personally, I couldn't see why praying together was so important to Jan. Obviously, I never verbalized this, for somehow I knew that this was not the right attitude for a husband to share with his wife.

Prayer became a larger part of my life when I entered the ministry, but I still perceived it as a task—part of what I was "supposed to do" as a pastor. I became comfortable praying with other people and in front of groups, even with our family, but still not with Jan. That just seemed too difficult. Someone described the process of a couple praying together as two people suddenly becoming naked spiritually with each other, and I related to that. My impression was that what Jan wanted me to do was to bare my soul before God in her presence. Later, I found out that wasn't her expectation at all, but when I wasn't willing even to talk about it, how was I to know?

Part of the problem was my personality. I typically need to take the time to process something internally before I can act upon it. I am the opposite of Jan in this. She needs to get something out—talk it out—in order to understand it. If I do that, I end up going in circles and it is very unproductive. So that compounded the problem, because every time she wanted to talk about it, I needed the time to think it through, to process it, and she thought I was rejecting her idea—and rejecting her.

So how did it all change? As we've worked on this chapter together, we've tried to remember the circumstances surrounding the change, but neither one of us can recall exactly what happened or when. All I know is that at some point soon after I left pastoral ministry to enter a counseling ministry, I "bit the bullet," so to speak, and agreed to pray with Jan, just the two of us.

I believe we started praying together during the time I was finishing my training as a counselor, and during one of my last courses, a group therapy class. As a part of that class, every student had to be involved in a group. Toward the end of the course, I had finally risked sharing some personal things with the group and had been pleasantly surprised when the negative response I had feared hadn't materialized. Instead of the judgment and condemnation I had expected, I had received the support and understanding of the other group members.

I remember coming home and sharing what had happened with Jan, and then getting up the courage to share some very personal things with her. As I did, I was fearful of what her response would be, and again I was pleasantly surprised. She was very loving and accepting of what I had shared. I believe it was during this period of time, and based on her response to my being vulnerable with her, that I finally took the risk and agreed to start praying with her. That was almost thirty years ago, and we've seldom missed a day since then. Even when one of us is traveling, we pray over the phone every day we are apart.

During the years that we have been praying together we

have experienced a spiritual intimacy which has seen us through the very worst of times in our marriage and family. Please don't think we know how to do it the only "right" way— to do so would be presumptive in our sharing about prayer. But we do hope that in sharing our struggle to keep prayer central in our relationship it will motivate and help those of you who want something more in your relationships with each other and in your relationships with God.

Richard Foster describes my struggle well. He says, "We today yearn for prayer and hide from prayer. We are attracted to it and repelled by it. We believe prayer is something we should do, even something we want to do, but it seems like a chasm stands between us and actually praying."[2] In my case, not only was there a struggle within me, there was a struggle between Jan and me, with Jan representing the yearning and me representing the hiding. Perhaps, as Foster goes on to say, I was waiting for everything to be "just right." Or perhaps I was waiting to become better at praying, or more willing to "pray deep." Whatever the reason, I do remember feeling like I just wasn't ready to do this "praying together" with Jan. I know now that part of my problem was that I was making everything too complicated. Neither Jan nor I knew how to get past the barriers until we just jumped in and began, with a few simple words.

Extraordinary Couples

JAN: Once we started praying together, Dave's objections simply went away. He found it wasn't as scary as he had thought.

The key for us was to begin in a very simple way. When we asked one couple how they got started praying together, they said, "We just opened our mouths and said, 'Dear Heavenly Father....'" At first reading, it seemed like they had missed the point of our question, but as we reflected on their response, we realized they were right on: keep it simple—just open your mouth and start.

Over the past couple of years, whenever we have been speaking to a group of couples, we have asked those who felt led to voluntarily commit to praying together every day for six weeks. More than four hundred couples have volunteered and made that commitment in writing, and many of them responded to a follow-up questionnaire about their experience of praying together. In this book, we want you to read about what they experienced as they prayed together daily.

There are too few voices today, against a cultural background of individualism, that continue to assert that the remedy for the distressed human condition and the ensuing inability to sustain human relationships is a spiritual one. Even when that call to a spiritual response is made, it is typically framed as an individual task. Sermons are preached, Sunday school lessons are taught, and books are written about what we can do to grow spiritually as individuals. Very little has been said or written about how we can respond to the call to a deepening spirituality, or to a growing prayer life, as a couple. We have found that spirituality can be developed to an even deeper level when it is approached not only individually, but also as a couple within the marriage relationship.

The onslaught of divorce tells the sad tale. As our culture has increasingly emphasized individualism, the divorce statistics have soared. Almost every divorce we have seen has happened because one or both people were caught up in the "meism" of our age. But it's a different story with couples who pray together. One couple, who work together in a marriage ministry involving many couples, shared in their response to our questionnaire that they had found that only one couple in 1,500 who pray together on a regular basis ever gets divorced.[3] That's quite a difference! Obviously, the couple who prays together stays together. Marital stability is clearly one of the things that results when couples pray together.

DAVE: I've tested this in my counseling work with couples, most of whom are in a time of crisis or a period of distress when they come to my office. As a part of their counseling, I sometimes ask them to discuss at home on a daily basis the problem that brought them into my office. Then I ask them, as a part of the "homework," to conclude every conversation about their problem, or about the crisis, by praying together, even if it's only a few simple words. I may even give them a simple prayer to read together. It's been amazing to see the changes that have taken place in those who have followed through and prayed together: attitudes have changed; behaviors have softened; and warm, caring feelings have had a chance to develop.

Throughout the book, we will share some of the responses to our questionnaire. One of the things we were looking for in the responses was how the experience of praying together affected each couple's sense of intimacy. One couple, who had already been praying together, wrote:

When we first started praying together over ten years ago, we didn't realize how close it would bring us to the Lord. It was a whole new arena of intimacy with him. But it was also a whole new arena of intimacy with each other—one we now consider as necessary to our relationship as oxygen is to our physical life.

They went on to describe how that happened for them. The husband said:

As we prayed together, I discovered for myself how important my wife's need for emotional sharing was. I found that I could use that need to lead us into some of our prayer focus. Over time, I've learned more about her heart and have seen us grow closer together through our mutual prayer time.

The wife added:

When we first started to pray together I was humbled to hear my husband's heart and how he wanted to walk closely with the Lord. Over the years I have felt closer and closer to my husband, the more we have prayed together. I know deep inside me that, although he is not perfect, he truly wants to be obedient to the Lord, and that is an awesome security for any wife.

What a powerful statement this couple makes about intimacy. They say they have found each other's hearts! So many couples don't know their partner's heart, and that lack of knowledge destroys the possibility of intimacy. Through praying together, however, the heart can be known. One wife said she tried to just forget her husband was there, and poured out her heart to the Lord. But of course, her husband was there, and as he listened, he could clearly hear her heart. When the heart is heard, intimacy is experienced.

Another couple wrote, "The Lord honored our time praying together and went ahead of us to do things we didn't even think to ask about, because 'The eyes of the Lord search the whole earth in order to strengthen those whose hearts are fully committed to him'" (2 Chr 16:9, NLT).

God was listening, and he heard not only the words they prayed, but also their hearts, and he responded to requests they couldn't even put into words. Many of the couples shared with us that during the six weeks they committed to pray together, a number of problems occurred in their marriages, or in their families, that earlier would have created dissension and distance between them. But because they were praying together, they were not only able to deal better with the issues, but they were also able to stay closer to each other.

Yet, lest you think that it was easy for those who committed to pray together, or think that all the responses were positive, let us be quick to say that we will also include the not-so-positive responses. Some couples reported negative experiences in their relationship when they committed themselves to pray together.

In the next chapter, we will look in more depth at the reasons why we need to pray together as couples. Then, in chapter three, we will look at some examples of couples who prayed together and experienced wonderful, clear answers to their prayers. Following that, in chapter four, we'll look at some couples who prayed together but found the answer to their prayers was "no." Some experienced disappointment, but others were able to find a different answer that satisfied.

Part two will look at the barriers encountered when couples have begun to pray together. Chapter five will look at the natural resistance couples have to praying together. Then, in chapter six, we'll discuss the specific barriers couples reported to us that made it impossible for them to follow through on their commitment to pray together. We also will address some of the emotional issues in a marriage that can perpetuate patterns that seem to prohibit the possibility of praying together. Chapter seven will look at how starting to pray together early in a relationship overcomes resistance and prepares us for the spiritual battles involved.

In part three, we will cover specific steps you can take at any stage of spiritual development to begin to pray together. Chapter eight will look at the importance of just getting started, and will include some ideas for how to pray together. In chapter nine, we will consider what to pray about when praying together. Throughout the book, we'll look at different couples' experiences as they prayed together. Chapter ten will share some stories of couples who experienced healing in their relationship as they prayed together. The final chapter will give you the opportunity to make a commitment in writing. There's something about writing it down that makes it more definite.

Basically, this book is an attempt to help couples find their own voice in the wilderness of our culture. It is a call for human transformation within marriage, the relationship that God created as the basic unit of commitment. We hope that as you read the responses that came from hundreds of couples—some who responded to our call for commitment to pray together for at least six weeks, and some who already pray together—it will trigger something in your heart that will give you the courage either to begin to pray together, or to do so more consistently. Perhaps you, or your spouse, has a heart that is yearning for spiritual intimacy but is held back by fear, or perhaps one of you is trying so hard to get the other motivated that resistance is deepened. If so, keep reading! We have included, at the end of each chapter, questions for discussion and sample prayers to get you started.

Questions to Discuss Together:

1. With whom do you identify more: Dave or Jan? Does one of you represent the yearning for praying together and one the hiding?
2. How important do you think prayer is in the life of the Christian?
3. Did you ever hear your parents pray? Do you know if they prayed together? Did you have prayer times together as a family? Did your parents ever tell you that they prayed for you?
4. What do you think is the main barrier to couples praying together?
5. Do any of your friends talk about praying together?
6. What kinds of prayer have you tried?

Prayers for Couples to Read and Pray Together:

~

Dear Heavenly Father:

We know how important it is to build a relationship with you through prayer, but we have hesitations about praying together. It seems so scary to both of us. It seems that when one of us is willing to talk about it the other resists. Or if we do talk about it all kinds of things come up that take our focus away from the subject of prayer. Will you help us through the maze of our lives so that we might be able to set aside just a few minutes to talk about prayer?

In the name of Jesus, Amen.

~

~

Dear Father in Heaven:

This prayer thing is very new to us. We hardly know how to pray by ourselves, let alone how to pray together as a couple. So we ask you to help us to not be intimidated by each other and to give us the courage to come into your presence as a couple. Together, we want to begin to build a strong, intimate relationship with you. We thank you in advance for your help.

In the name of Jesus we ask this, Amen.

~

~

Dear Father God:

We are challenged by the idea of praying together. We enjoy being able to talk with you on our own, and we feel very privileged to be welcomed into your presence individually. We want to do this as a couple together, and so we ask that you will help us to be as diligent in learning how to pray together as we have tried to be in our own personal life of prayer with you. Help us to find the time. Help us to overcome our shyness, or our fears about talking to you with our partner beside us. We look forward to what you are going to do in our marriage as we seek to be faithful in developing intimacy with you as a couple.

Thank you for caring about us so much.

In the name of Jesus we ask this, Amen.

~

Chapter Two

THE POWER OF TWO

If two of you agree down here on earth concerning anything you ask, my Father in heaven will do it for you. For where two or three gather together because they are mine, I am there among them.

MATTHEW 18:19-20, NLT

DAVE: Silence. It was almost unbearable. The two of us sat there so burdened, so hurt, so angry we could not speak. We had been there before, but the familiarity of the feelings was no comfort. Our teenage son was missing—again! This time, for certain, we would handle it correctly. Every other time we had faced a crisis with this particular son, we had fought about what to do. Jan usually seemed to want to do something, while I said there wasn't anything more to do. Other times we switched roles, as Jan gave up trying and I panicked, thinking surely there was something we should be doing. All the while we desperately wanted God to act.

I don't think our marriage would have stayed together during those desperate years had it not been for our commitment to praying together daily. Our prayer time became the settling point in our turmoil—the time for the evening-out of emotions that so easily went out of control. Through that time, God began something in us both that has lasted a lifetime.

He certainly didn't do it "our" way, but all through those dark times, God was at work. On our end, we questioned, argued with God, and angrily endured his silence, and then together in prayer we calmed down and once again recognized that he was there. Our acknowledgment of his sovereignty in our time of prayer together gradually created within each of us a new mind-set. That didn't mean the battle was over, but we were once again able to know God was in control and at work. And when one of us started to lose our perspective, praying together brought it back. It was much later than we expected or thought it should be when God acted in our son's life. God did it his way and in his time, and it was marvelous to see it when it happened. What sustained us in the "in-between" time was our prayer times together.

Maybe you are where we were then. I can't think of a better reason to begin praying together. It's never too late or too early to start! You can start in a crisis, but it's even better to start praying together before those times of crisis come, in order to get your hearts in sync with God's heart. We were grateful that we had already begun the process of praying together before the problems with our son hit us. I don't know if we would have had the discipline to begin once it had started. Start now.

Praying Together

A good starting point for understanding why it is so important to pray together is to look at Jesus' words in Matthew 18. What did Jesus mean when he said, "If two of you agree down here on earth concerning anything you ask, my Father in heaven will do it for you"? We know that there are many times when two people agree before the Lord about someone's physical healing, or someone's spiritual conversion, or that circumstances must change, yet the prayer isn't answered in the literal sense.

These are Jesus' words, however, so there must be importance to what he is saying, and there must also be an amazing depth of meaning to his words. To begin, William Barclay points out in his commentary on Matthew that Jesus is clearly teaching us in this passage that "prayer must never be selfish, and that selfish prayer cannot find an answer. We are not meant to pray ... thinking of nothing and no one but ourselves; we are meant to pray as members of a fellowship, in agreement, remembering that life and the world are not arranged for us as individuals, but for the fellowship as a whole."[4] That's a good point for us, living in such an individualistic world. Barclay goes on to make the point that no matter the size of the group, Jesus is present. Even though he doesn't mention the married couple specifically, it still applies to us as a couple. He says that Jesus "is there whenever faithful hearts meet, however few they may be."[5]

The second thing we see in this passage is that our Lord tells us there is incredible power available to us when we pray together. There is spiritual strength in uniting together to do spiritual battle. This is true not just when we have hundreds gathered together, but also when there are only two who agree together. Obviously that power doesn't mean we can dictate to God what he is to do simply by our joining together in prayer. He is still sovereign, and his answers may not match our requests and our desires.

JAN: We experienced frustration even when we as a couple agreed together over the years regarding the problems Dave has already mentioned with one of our children. We not only agreed together in prayer, we worked hard to arrange circumstances so that God could work his miracle. When the results didn't match our desires and our requests, we were angry and disappointed with God. One of the hardest lessons we had to learn was that God is God, and just because we held on to a literal interpretation of a verse in the Bible, that didn't make us sovereign. God answered, but in his own way and in his own time. We've learned over the years that there is great power in agreeing together in prayer, but God is still in control, and he hears, and he will answer, giving us what we need even though it may be different from the literal desire of our request.

Many of us think of these verses when we grab a friend and ask him or her to agree with us in prayer. That's part of the promise Jesus is giving us here. But why not start with the most basic "twosome" in our lives? Think of this promise in relation to praying and agreeing together with your spouse. That same incredible power given to those who pray together is available to couples when they agree together in prayer. Several couples noted in their responses to our questionnaire that through praying together as a couple they had experienced a number of remarkable answers to prayer. One couple said, "When we first started to pray together some years ago, we were amazed, not only at the spiritual oneness we felt, but also at the answered prayers we experienced."

Another couple wrote in response to the question, "Did you

experience any 'surprises' in the process of praying together?": "Yes—God answered my prayer request—a big one—in a way that I never expected! We had a major problem in our business, and I thought I had figured out a way to solve it, but God had a better idea and his solution didn't even involve me—God worked out the resolution his way!"

From some of the comments couples made, it seemed they felt that when a husband and wife were in agreement in prayer, it strengthened their effectiveness. In truth, God pays close attention to the prayers of each of his children, but we are also warned about what happens when we are not in agreement as a husband and wife. The word *agree* is "derived from a Greek word from which we get our English word 'symphony.' It means 'to be in accord or harmony' or 'to make one mind.'"[6] This takes on added meaning when we think of it in terms of husbands and wives being in "harmony" as they pray. Peter presses this point when he writes to husbands regarding their wives, "If you don't treat her as you should, your prayers will not get ready answers" (1 Pt 3:7, TLB). Thus, the Bible seems to say that answered prayer in a marriage relationship will be based on agreement—harmony—between the husband and wife.

Spiritual Intimacy

Praying together is a part of how we develop spiritual intimacy in a marriage. If we go back to the beginning, it is interesting to note that God did not make Eve out of the dust of the earth, as he had made Adam. Instead, God made Eve from a part of

Adam, causing Adam to exclaim when he first saw her, "At last!... She is part of my own flesh and bone" (Gn 2:23, NLT). The writer then goes on to describe marriage as the reason, "why a man leaves his father and mother and is joined to his wife, and the two are united into one" (v. 24). The mystery of marriage is how we can experience a total union that encompasses all—body, mind, emotions, soul, and spirit—yet still be separate individuals. That's the mystery of intimacy, and that's what God intended for us to experience.

When we hear the word "intimacy," many people think we are talking only about physical intimacy. That is a part of intimacy, but there are nine other areas of intimacy that have been identified. They include:

1. Emotional intimacy (we tune in to what we are each feeling)
2. Intellectual intimacy (we share ideas together)
3. Social intimacy (we enjoy each other in social settings)
4. Recreational intimacy (the shared experiences of fun and play)
5. Creative intimacy (sharing in the creation of things)
6. Crisis intimacy (the closeness we experience as we together cope with problems and painful things in our lives)
7. Work intimacy (sharing in common tasks)
8. Conflict intimacy (a sense of closeness by facing and struggling together with our differences)
9. Spiritual intimacy

All of these types of intimacy interact with each other in the development of a relationship.

To better understand the meaning of spiritual intimacy, it helps to go back to the Garden of Eden as it was experienced in Genesis 2—before sin entered the picture. We can imagine that in the absence of fear and shame, Adam and Eve experienced a wonderful openness with each other. In addition, they shared that same openness with God. In the evening, God came and walked with them through the garden. As they walked together, they probably shared their day with God, and they experienced a special closeness with God.

Now, I don't believe God came and walked with them each individually during the evening. The sense of the passage is that this was something they shared together with God. This kind of openness with each other and in their relationship with God was the way marriage was designed to be.

But sin entered the picture as Adam and Eve rebelled and were disobedient. We read, "The fruit looked so fresh and delicious, and it would make her so wise! So she ate some of the fruit. She also gave some to her husband, who was with her. Then he ate it, too. At that moment, their eyes were opened, and they suddenly felt shame at their nakedness" (Gn 3:6-7, NLT). In addition, they felt guilt and fear, for they hid themselves, not wanting to walk with God that evening. In their discussion with God about what they had done, they were for the first time defensive, blaming each other for what they had willfully done.

Now, instead of openness, Adam and Eve experienced shame, guilt, fear, and defensiveness in their relationships with each other and with God. Because of these negative factors, which affect all human relationships, and especially marriage, many writers and teachers have suggested that marriage is too complicated a relationship for spiritual intimacy to take place.[7] Perhaps this is why so little has been written about spiritual intimacy in marriage.

We have found that a sense of spiritual intimacy is gained as we, as a couple, seek to restore in our marriage those things that were lost for Adam and Eve back in Genesis. We want to regularly confront not only the shame, defensiveness, and fear that any two people are going to encounter in a marriage, but also seek to repair the brokenness that came as a result of sin, between us as a couple and in our relationship with God.

Although we cannot go back to the innocence Adam and Eve had in the garden before the Fall, we can seek to restore to some degree the spiritual intimacy they shared with God, both as a couple and as individuals. We want to recapture some of the joy they must have experienced through their shared intimacy with God.

A number of couples commented on the fact that as they prayed together and built a greater sense of spiritual intimacy, they also were able to experience a greater sense of physical intimacy. One wife summed it up best when she wrote: "We have found that since we have been praying together, our prayer time has definitely enhanced our physical intimacy as well. We both feel more satisfied and have learned to respect each other's needs."

This is really not that surprising. Physical intimacy is, at its most basic level, a beautiful form of communication. If a husband and wife are not communicating verbally, that lack of communication will soon affect their physical relationship.

Dave has found in counseling couples that many times, sexual difficulties in a marriage are resolved as a couple learns how to better communicate verbally. What many couples reported to us was that through praying together daily, they were able to open areas of communication with each other that had been blocked previously. Enhanced sexual intimacy is sure to follow. That was a surprise to a number of couples.

Spiritual intimacy is earlier promised in the verses quoted from Matthew 18, especially verse 20. Jesus said, "Where two or three come together in my name, there am I with them" (NIV). God in our presence—what an incredible privilege. The Jews have a similar saying: "Where two sit and are occupied with the study of the Law, the glory of God is among them."[8] When a couple kneels to pray together, the glory of God is there with them! What an awesome, intimate, glorious occasion!

Spiritual Intimacy Builds Trust

The issue of trust enters the counseling office with almost every troubled couple. As trust has eroded, so has their intimacy. For any type of intimacy to exist in a relationship, those involved need to be able to trust each other. Intimacy builds upon a foundation of trust. But it is equally true that shared intimacy helps to build trust. In many ways, intimacy and trust are interwoven.

We have found that one of the most important blessings that has come out of our praying together is a deepening of our trust for each other. Many of the couples who have written us say the same thing. You can hear it in their stories. An example of this is what Gary J. Oliver, the executive director of the Center for Marriage and Family Studies at John Brown University shared in an interview in the March-April 1999 issue of *Ministries Today* magazine:

> If there is one thing that has transformed our marriage relationship it has been to regularly and faithfully pray together. When Carrie and I pray together, I know her heart, and she knows my heart. And that has built a trust. And trust trusts every day, week by week.
>
> We get up early every morning to pray together, and I'm not a morning person. Our praying together has affected all kinds of things in our relationship, including communication. But the main thing we've experienced is the growth of trust with each other, and trust is an absolutely essential ingredient for intimacy. No trust, no intimacy.

Spiritual Intimacy Is Always Intentional

In some areas of our lives, growth occurs naturally—it is simply a function of time. For example, we grow older physically, no matter what we do to try to stop the process. A child's body grows into an adult body. But when it comes to growth in an area such as spirituality, it never "just happens." We have to plan it and make it happen. We have to make a choice to be obedient to what God has told us to do in order to experience spiritual growth; doing things such as reading the Bible, praying, and worshiping with other believers. One of the primary things Jesus taught his disciples was the importance of obedience. Obedience is always a choice—it is always intentional.

This is just as true when it comes to developing spiritual intimacy in our marriage. I think many couples assume that if each of them is growing spiritually as an individual, then spiritual intimacy in the marriage will naturally follow. That assumption prevents us from understanding that the same process at work in us individually must also take place in us as a couple. We must begin with mutual obedience, which creates the discipline, and then together we can develop the behaviors that bring about growth, including praying together.

But It's Still Difficult

Achieving spiritual intimacy is difficult, not only because of the shame, fear, and defensiveness that resulted from the Fall, but also because there are basic differences in the way men and women approach a subject like spiritual intimacy. To begin with, men tend to be "fixers" while women tend to be "listeners and talkers." You can easily see the developing problem— what is there about spiritual intimacy that a man can "fix"? Nothing!

One wife wrote, "I didn't feel very safe praying with my husband. I'd talk to God and my husband would later try to 'fix' whatever it was I was praying about. I think that's a natural response, but not the right thing to do. He is very careful now just to listen."

Obviously, listening and talking together with God develop intimacy. This is something that, as this wife noted, usually comes more naturally to women. Most men thus begin this process from a one-down position, which naturally stirs up more shame, fear, and defensiveness. When a man experiences those emotions, his natural tendency is to withdraw and go off somewhere by himself, either literally or in his head, to think about a solution.

In comparison, look at what happens when a woman experiences fear, shame, and defensiveness. She usually wants to talk about it with someone who will listen, which is a natural part of the way we develop intimacy. If her husband can join her in that process and they can include God in the equation, they will be developing spiritual intimacy. The two essential ingredients for any kind of intimacy, including spiritual intimacy, are a willingness to share what is going on in one's life and a willingness to become vulnerable with the other person. Unfortunately, both husband and wife get in the way. Usually the one wanting to talk (this is usually the woman but sometimes the husband) pressures the other, making that one feel frustrated, guilty, and defensive, thus squelching any hope of spiritual intimacy.

The Role of Fear

You can see that in either the husband or wife, a willingness to share, and especially a willingness to be vulnerable, are contradictory to our fears. We may be willing to be obedient out of fear, and we may even be submissive out of fear, but we will never allow ourselves to be vulnerable out of fear. Fear stops any sense of vulnerability and shuts down any possibility of sharing anything close to our heart with our spouse. Only when we have broken the power of our fear can we discover the freedom to together "come boldly to the very throne of God and stay there to receive his mercy and to find grace to help us in our times of need" (Heb 4:16, TLB).

When fear still has its hold on our hearts, it pushes us away from other people. We find all kinds of ways to avoid confronting that fear. Busyness is one of the common ways we withdraw from another person. It's difficult to get through to someone who is avoiding us through busyness. After all, what that person is busy doing is probably something that needs to be done.

Sometimes fear causes us to push another person away through our irritability. Have you ever noticed how easy it is to focus on some irritating behavior in your spouse when you are having a discussion about something that you aren't comfortable talking about? Or you get a feeling of restlessness, or just an overall feeling of unease that causes you to avoid what, on the surface, you seem to want. Resistance is also born out of fear, and we'll spend all of chapter five looking at how it relates to our praying together.

What If Only One of Us Is Interested?

The place to begin when only one of you is interested in praying together is to consider the possibility that your spouse's real issue is one of fear. The partner who uses anger or silence whenever the subject of praying together is brought up may be using these tactics to cover up the fact that he or she is afraid. Any behavior exhibited by a spouse that increases the feeling of distance between the partners is usually motivated by fear. If we respond only to the anger, or the silence, we may miss the real issue.

Check it out. If your spouse is angry, or silent, or rejecting, ask him or her something like this: "I can see you really are upset (or, don't want to talk about this). Is it because you are uncomfortable (another way to describe fear) with what we are talking about?" When you can make the distinction between the response you can see on the surface and the fear you suspect lies beneath the surface, both of you can respond differently.

If fear isn't the issue, and your spouse just isn't interested in spiritual things, it is important to remember the apostle Peter's words. Even though what he says is directed to wives, it applies equally to husbands in the same situation. He says, "Wives, fit in with your husbands' plans; for then if they refuse to listen when you talk to them about the Lord, they will be won by your respectful, pure behavior. Your godly lives will speak to them better than any words" (1 Pt 3:1-2, TLB).

DAVE: I recall a time when Jan and I were not in agreement on some major issues, and she said to me, "You go ahead and do what you want, but I'm going to work on being more of God's woman." That was all she said on the subject, but did she ever get my attention! When your partner is not on the same page with you in your desire for spiritual intimacy, work on your own relationship with the Lord, and entrust your spouse's participation to God.

What If One of Us Isn't a Believer?

One wife whose husband volunteered them to pray together daily for six weeks wrote back on the questionnaire that her husband was not a believer and that she was totally surprised by his willingness to volunteer to pray together. She followed his lead, and they prayed together every day for the six weeks.

He wrote: "I'm not a true Christian (that is, I do not view Jesus as my Lord and Savior), but I am spiritual. This means I seek to have a sense of myself and my place in the universe. Praying with my wife has helped me to be even more in touch with this aspect of my life."

His wife added: "I really appreciate his effort. I would love for this to be an area we can both share in our lives. Up until now, our religious faith has been an area that we lived separately."

Who knows what God is going to do in this couple's lives as they open themselves to him! The process of building spiritual intimacy in our marriage is grounded in a common obedience to God, who is our focus. Couples who pray are meeting with the Lord of the universe—Jesus Christ. Communion together is our goal, and it is a lifetime process we can share as a couple. It takes only one to build a relationship with God, but there is a special power when there are two of us involved in that process.

In chapter eight we will provide some specific suggestions on how to get started, but first, let's look at some of the things couples have learned as they have started or continued the process of regularly praying together.

Questions to Discuss Together:

1. Read together the passage of Scripture quoted at the beginning of the chapter (Mt 18:19-20). What do you think Jesus meant when he talked about the agreement of two or more?
2. Why do you think it is important for a husband and wife to agree in prayer?
3. What kind of relationship do you think Adam and Eve had with God before they disobeyed him? As they walked in the garden with God what can you imagine they talked about?
4. What do you think is meant by the phrase *spiritual intimacy?*
5. What do you think it means to hear another's heart?
6. Can you think of any specific answers you have had to your individual prayers? Talk about them with each other. Do you know of specific answers to prayer any of your friends or family have had?

Prayers for Couples to Read and Pray Together:

~

Dear Heavenly Father:

You wrote in your Word that is important for two or three to agree together, and that if they did you would be there with them. We have a hard time agreeing on much of anything, but we are interested in finding out more about what you meant when you said that. Help us to get our schedules in sync so that we can talk to each other about this. Show us why it is important for us to pray together. Our lives are so fragmented and hectic that we are not sure this would work for us. We need you to help us with that. Would you give us a quiet spirit so that we can have clear thoughts about you and what you want for us as a couple?

In the name of Jesus, Amen.

~

Dear Father in Heaven:

There are a lot of things in our life we agree upon, and there are some things where we have trouble agreeing. Perhaps we need to hear each other's heart more. We ask that you help us slow down and listen better to each other. Give us the ability to understand each other better and help us to be slower in speaking and reacting to the other so that we can begin to take the time needed for listening. And in those areas of our life where we do agree, we come to you in agreement about some of these things: (List them). Thank you for listening to us. It's hard to believe that you care so much for us that you wait patiently for us to come to you and that you love to listen to us. We thank you for that.

In the name of Jesus, Amen.

~

Dear Father God:

We never really thought about this idea of agreeing together in prayer as being important to us as a couple. We've only thought about it in relation to others. How clear it is now that it also includes us as a couple. From this point on, God, you're going to hear about things from us together. And we are going to work on being in agreement, not just about the things we are asking you for, but also we are going to work at being in agreement about our life together as a couple. We want to have this strength in our marriage and we want to have this power in our relationship with you. How exciting it is to know that you want that for us too, and that you have promised to meet together with us when we are in agreement. Thanks so much for your promises! We want to learn how to express our love to you and let you be even more involved with us in our marriage.

In the name of Jesus we pray this, Amen.

~

Chapter Three

PRAYING AND THE RAIN CAME

Elijah was as human as we are, and yet when he prayed earnestly that no rain would fall, none fell for the next three and a half years! Then he prayed for rain, and down it poured. The grass turned green, and the crops began to grow again.

JAMES 5:17-18, NLT

James is describing the passage in 1 Kings 17 where Elijah told King Ahab that because of the king's evil ways, there would be a time of trouble—no rain or dew. The time of drought would continue until Elijah prayed for it to end. Everything happened as he said it would. There are definitely times when it seems as if the thing we pray for comes about and God intervenes in our time of trouble. He may not respond as quickly as he did to Elijah, but the answer is clear for all to see.

We've already referred to the comments couples have made about how their commitment to pray together has helped them through tough times. One couple, whose commitment to pray together started right after Thanksgiving, said that this was the first Christmas season they had not experienced conflict as a couple, and they felt it was directly due to the fact that they were praying together each day during December.

Another couple said, "Our daily prayer time held us together as a couple through devastating circumstances." Shared prayer has provided a bond for these couples, stronger than any outside circumstance.

Other couples told of specific answers to their prayers.

Les and Leslie

Les and Leslie Parrott direct the Center for Relationship Development at Seattle Pacific University, and are friends of ours. When their first baby was born prematurely, weighing only fifteen ounces, people all over the country joined in praying for little John Leslie. We remember Les telling us how his wedding ring could fit all the way up little John's arm. We could not even comprehend a baby that small. How could a little one that size survive? We readily agreed to pray for him. Les agreed to write the story of how praying together sustained them during this traumatic time:

As any couple who has experienced a tumultuous pregnancy or a crisis with an infant or child knows, the vulnerability you feel as a parent is almost beyond description. Without the gift of prayer we cannot imagine how we could have sustained our shared strength. There have been many times in our married life when prayer didn't feel like a gift—when our praying together seemed to symbolize our differences in style and need. But the moments of crisis with baby John pushed us into shared prayer, even if it felt awkward or uncomfortable, when one or both of us might not have felt much like praying, even when the words that spilled out fell flat rather than expressing the desires of our heart. Our need for prayer overcame all the resistance and kept us praying our imperfect prayers. There were moments so immense they literally drove us to our knees.

So many points in our crisis could not have been survived without shared prayer: the day Leslie was wheeled directly from the doctor's office to the hospital for what was to be the remainder of the pregnancy; the doctor's announcement that the decision to deliver at twenty-eight weeks was unavoidable; the phone call in the early morning hours summoning us to the hospital for John's emergency surgery when he weighed barely one pound; the dreaded news of a brain bleed; a collapsed lung; a serious eye disease. Each of these moments required a focused strength not possible without God's presence.

There were also the moments of gratitude so rich that we understood how Christ felt when he said, "if these people don't praise God, the very rocks will cry out in praise." It was 11:30 P.M. on Sunday evening, February 28, 1998, when John's postoperative body finally pulled out of severe shock and the monitors fell to safer levels while he lapsed into sleep after five days of terrifying pain and fragility. July 11, 1998, was the day an intricate eye exam revealed John's deteriorating eyesight was stabilizing and had actually begun a healing process that would reverse the current damage. The immensity of gratitude that filled our marriage in these moments, and the prayers of simple thanksgiving we shared, transformed any remnant of feeling that prayer was a duty for us to perform rather than a power that enables us to live in God's presence.

By far, the most important times of prayer we have experienced as a couple have been the most unremarkable ones—conversations in the car, for example, that turned into prayers. Throughout the months John was hospitalized, the daily drives to the hospital became occasions for much prayer. These times of prayer were sometimes interspersed with impatient comments like, "Why did you have to make that last phone call? Because of you we might miss John's feeding time!" or with jealous surges like, "I get to hold John today since you got to hold him last night."

Through the months that followed John's homecoming—months filled with the ordinary days of severe colic, constant crying, projectile vomiting, and a baby tethered to an oxygen tank—it was shared prayer that entered our drama of needs, drives, and desires and gave us the strength to come closer to self-giving love. Did we achieve perfection? Not exactly. But that's what keeps us coming back together to shared times of honest prayer.

It's hard to imagine how couples make it through experiences like Les and Leslie's without the strength they receive from the Lord through praying together. Little John is getting bigger and is through most of the tough times now, but the struggle is not over completely yet, and Les and Leslie know where to find the strength for the reparative work that's still to be done.

Don and Luciana

Don and Luciana Struthers are a special couple we met in Gauteng, South Africa. They are each in their second marriage, and when they tried to blend their families, chaos came along with the process, especially with Luciana's youngest daughter. For a while it seemed Don and Luciana's marriage was headed for trouble. Don tells their story:

I'm sure most people have experienced that the Lord usually responds to prayer in one of three ways—either "yes," "no," or "wait"—depending on the circumstances and the condition of our hearts at the time. While we both prefer to have a request granted immediately, Luciana and I have learned to appreciate the abundant grace that God provides when his answer seems to be a flat "no" or "wait just awhile." We've also noticed that his replies to our prayers about our children's welfare seldom come at once. Those answers come over an extended period of time, during which he lovingly teaches us to develop patience, perseverance, and to align ourselves with his will instead of our own.

We were married in 1980, each for the second time— Luciana with three children and I with two children from our first marriages. The adjustment to a new family was not easy for any of us, and was aggravated by the fact that I had suffered with a drinking problem on and off for most of my adult life.

In 1984, Luciana and I both accepted the Lord Jesus as our Savior, and we started praying together every day from that point on. Luciana's middle child had received Jesus as her Savior at the young age of twelve, and it was in answer to her faithful prayers over several years that her mom and I finally came to know the Lord. The initial concern of our joint prayers was for the safety of our youngest child—Luciana's daughter, who was in her early teens at the time.

During a conflict with her, she left our home without informing anyone of her plans or destination. As newly saved babes, it was the first real heartache that Luciana and I took to the Lord in prayer together. Some of the background to that problem will illustrate how our praying together was then—and still is today—a point of real strength for ourselves and now for all our children.

Although the Lord helped me to overcome my addiction to alcohol right from the time of my salvation, my ability to relate to the family did not improve as quickly as we would have liked. This was probably the main reason why Luciana's youngest was drawn into the company of some unruly and rebellious kids.

It was a Thursday night when she left home, and of course, mom, brother, sister, the natural father, and I were equally devastated. Our prayers were not only for her safety, but also for grace and wisdom in knowing where to begin the search. Calls to friends, visits to places where we thought she might be during that night and throughout the next day brought no results.

By Saturday morning we were all frantic, and realized that in the chaos we hadn't taken the time to pray together. Luciana and I knelt together at our bedside and poured our hearts out before the Lord in tears and supplication. As we did, it was as if the "peace which passes all understanding" that Paul speaks about in Philippians 4:7 came over us as we carried the burden to the Lord in prayer and resolutely agreed to leave it in his loving care without taking it back. We've found that our praying together helps us leave the burden with the Lord!

You can easily imagine the extent of the joy that entered our souls when our daughter phoned about half an hour later. She was not willing to say where she was, but just that she had realized we would be worried, and had decided to phone and at least say that she was safe. What a relief to hear those words! We were filled with thanksgiving, knowing that it was the Lord who had prompted her to call in answer to our prayers.

The problems were by no means over. Our little darling had gotten mixed up with some older kids who were on drugs, and when we did eventually track them down, there was a need for some serious confrontations with several of them. Over the next several years, there were many other times when Luciana and I had to seek comfort, wisdom, and strength from the Lord together.

The situation started to improve only after one really unpleasant incident. Once again, our daughter left home, this time to move in with an addict "friend" against our wishes. This time we found as we prayed together that the Lord gave us the extra courage we needed to take a really tough stand about her relationships, and to have faith that he would bring about the necessary changes instead of allowing us to continue to fail by doing it our way. When she returned home after about ten days to collect some belongings, Luciana reminded her firmly that it had been her choice to move out, and insisted that she get straight back to wherever she was staying. The shock of the change that the Lord had enabled us to make toward her poor behavior had an impact on her and she returned home several days later with a repentant heart and a much better attitude.

God's progressive answers to our joint prayers are now evident in the life of our daughter, who was one of the few amongst her friends who came out of those adolescent escapades without any permanent scars. One of her friends during that rebellious time died a couple of years later of an overdose, and another one, whom I've come to know through a recovery ministry, is still struggling. We not only rejoice in the Lord's protection of Luciana's daughter, but were thrilled when a few years after the change in her attitudes and behaviors, she received the Lord Jesus as her own personal Savior.

Today, Luciana's three children, my two children, many of their friends, and even our respective ex-spouses have accepted the Lord as their Savior. I have become progressively more involved in a Bible-based outreach and training program for people caught up in substance abuse—mainly out of gratitude for what God has done in my own life, but also because I want to help others avoid the same mistakes that I made as an alcoholic, a husband, and a parent.

Luciana and I were further blessed with a son of our own seven years ago, and the way in which God has ministered his love as our heavenly Father to us through this child is yet another miracle. It is a perfect example of God's faithfulness in responding not only to our individual prayers, but, it seems to us, especially to our joint prayers.

We're able to pray to God with much thanksgiving, and to accept that when he does not say "yes" immediately, it just means that he wants us to persevere and to wait patiently upon him for a while longer. It is during those times of waiting that we have learned so many things of value for our life together here on earth—and also for a more meaningful purpose that will be revealed clearly only on the day when Jesus returns to take us to our eternal home in heaven above.

Don and Luciana were able to see God answer their prayers. They also found that praying together was a source of real strength, not only in their marriage, but in their family as well. The answers came—just not in their time frame.

Ray and Lois

Here's the story of a couple who found that praying together became the catalyst for healing in their broken marriage. Ray and Lois had been married for more than thirty years when Ray suddenly seemed to change.

Lois described what happened:

I guess he had a midlife crash, not just a crisis. He started spending time with some friends I had never met before. He started having some unexplained blocks of time, and if I asked him about it, he became angry. I couldn't believe what was happening to Ray. He was changing right before my eyes. For years, we had worked in ministry together. He taught the young couples' class at church, and loved it. We were both involved with those couples. I think when he gave up teaching that class was when I knew something fishy was going on.

Then when Lois discovered that one of Ray's main activities with his new friends was visiting topless bars and strip clubs, she asked him to move out.

For some time, Ray didn't seem to grasp the seriousness of the problem. But after about six months of living on his own, Ray began spending some time with his pastor, and then got himself into counseling. Here's what he had to say:

A lot of the problem was my pride and stubbornness. I just couldn't get the picture of what Lois was feeling. It didn't seem like such a big deal. We were just having some fun—a little adolescent, maybe, but not what Lois seemed to make of it.

Anyway, when I started talking with my pastor, he helped me see that even if I didn't think it was a big deal, the fact that Lois did made it a big deal. And then he almost casually said, "Why don't you and Lois spend some time praying together?" I almost didn't even catch what he said, but at that point, my pride was in the gutter and my stubbornness had gotten me nowhere. I was ready to try anything!

When the counselor suggested that we start spending some time together, I suggested that we pray together each time before I left. I still chuckle inside when I think of the look on Lois' face. She didn't know whether to be pleased, or to think that this was just some temporary strategy for me to get back into the house.

Maybe it was that look on Lois' face, but suddenly I was determined to follow through on this praying together thing. As we started spending more time together, I really started to look forward to our prayer time. There was a special intimacy there that I hadn't experienced before. With the regularity of our praying together, there was also a more consistent flow of information about things that really mattered—people at work, saying or doing something that hurt me, sharing joys of our children, or coping with the challenges of our relationship in more mature ways.

The other thing that really helped me was listening to the hurt in Lois as she prayed about our marriage. It was almost like I could hear her heart when she was talking to the Lord—and I couldn't do that when she talked directly to me about those same things. But it was broader than that. I think I was able to also hear her other emotional needs. I think it really helped me to know her better. And I'm sure it was a key to our getting back together again. We pray together every day now.

Lois agreed with what Ray said, adding:

Our prayer times often led to long conversations in which Ray was very open and honest with me. He'd typically been the silent thinker type. I used to learn more about him listening to him teach the couples' Sunday school class than I ever did from any of our conversations. But when we started praying together while we were separated, I felt like

I finally got to really know my husband. Not only did I get a clearer picture of his relationship with God, I was also able to learn more about his fears, his inadequacies, and, generally, what was in his mind.

It helped a lot in my learning to trust him again. The first thing I had to believe was that the changes he was making in our relationship—the praying together—were real, and that this wasn't just a way to get back into the house. It took a couple of months, and then I took the risk and invited him back home. I was really afraid that we would just slide back to the way things used to be, but our counselor helped me see that the only way I was going to know if the changes were real was to move forward.

It's been four years now since Ray went off the deep end, so that means it's been a little over three-and-a-half years since we started praying together. I don't know if we'd be back together if we hadn't started praying together. It's those times of prayer that keep us on the same page, rather than guessing, or hoping, what the other might be feeling or thinking. Each time we hold hands and pray, I feel secure, trusting, and very intimate with Ray.

More Success Stories

Other couples echoed Ray's and Lois' words. Joe and Sharon attended a retreat we led, and Joe wrote:

I felt that your challenge to pray together was the most important thing for me out of the whole weekend. It made

Sharon and me realize we had drifted away from some important habits we had when we first were married—to spend time in God's Word and to pray together. I also realized that as a result, we had drifted apart. Even though I teach an adult Bible class, and lead a home Bible study, it was so powerful to realize that for Sharon it felt like I was ignoring her by not regularly talking and praying together. Thank you for allowing God to remind me of that important truth.

Sue and Mark found that praying together wasn't easy at the beginning. After making the six-week commitment, it took them seven weeks to get started. But once they started, they observed, "praying together makes us conscious of God's working in our lives. It has made us a stronger 'couple' in being able to stand up for what is right and to walk righteously together. Before, we knew God led and blessed us, but now it seems we're more aware of his activity in our life together."

Another couple said, "We see ourselves coping better with stress amidst different family situations. We've seen answers to prayer for our children and ourselves. We've also become less fearful of judgment from our partner and more intimate about ourselves and our thoughts. It's been a real building experience."

Many couples experienced surprise at the answers they received to their prayers as they prayed together. Some felt that God had answered their individual prayers just as often, but because these prayers hadn't been shared with their partners, they didn't share the answers to prayer, and so weren't as aware of those answers. These couples found that praying together gave them a greater awareness of God's activity in their lives because not only did they pray together, they also talked about the answers to those prayers.

Others affirmed that there was more power in their praying because they were doing it together. In some special way, they realized the reality of Jesus' words quoted earlier, "Where two or three are gathered in my name, there I am in the midst of them." One couple remarked that God had worked in areas of their life that they weren't even praying about. Other couples said things like, "We really felt God in our midst," and, "After praying together, we have a real sense of God's presence in our marriage and our family." One husband said, "Hearing my wife pray showed me a whole different perspective of God."

We know that God meets each couple in a special way when they commit to meet consistently together with God in prayer. But, as with everything else in the Christian life, following a "formula" does not mean that the outcome is guaranteed to be what we want. The next chapter looks at what has happened for couples when the "rain didn't come."

Questions to Discuss Together:

1. Read together the passage quoted at the beginning of the chapter (Jas 5:17-18). Then talk together about what you think gave Elijah the courage and the boldness to ask for rain to come.

2. Do you think it is OK to ask God for specific things, or to ask him to change circumstances?

3. Do you think God hears every prayer that is prayed?
4. Why do you think some people seem to get specific answers while others do not?

Prayers for Couples to Read and Pray Together:

Dear Heavenly Father:

We know that other people talk about their answers to prayer, but we have not had that experience. Do you really hear us every time we cry out to you? We have gone through some pretty tough times and we have had times when we have doubted that you even cared about us. Help us to know you better. Help us to learn how you work, and specifically how you can work in our circumstances. We need to know that. We have some doubts about whether you choose to intervene in situations, and our faith is weak in some areas. We want to build our faith, but we do not know exactly how to do that. Give us guidance, we pray.

In the name of Jesus, Amen.

~

Dear Father in Heaven:

Sometimes we are hurting so much that we don't even want to pray. We feel like you are so far away that you can't hear us anyway. Where do you go? Or is it that we have gone away from you? We don't want to do that, but sometimes our situation is so painful we withdraw from everyone. Help us to learn how to stay closer to you in those difficult times. Help us to learn how to better help each other during those times. We want to be stronger in our relationship with each other, and in our relationship with you. Help us to be aware of your presence with us in the difficult times, when they come. Thank you that we can ask this of you and that you understand our hearts even better than we do.

In the name of Jesus, Amen.

~

Dear Father God:

As we talked together and looked back over our marriage, we do see your activity in our lives during those difficult times. We weren't so certain you were there when the difficult times were upon us, but in hindsight, and in faith, we know you were walking alongside us and that you cared about the pain we were experiencing. We didn't like those difficult times, but we don't know how else we could have learned so much about you, about ourselves, and about each other. We'd like to pray that you would keep us free from those difficult times, but we also know that wouldn't be realistic—life doesn't work that way. What we do pray is that we would see your hand at work; that we would sense your presence; and that our hearts would trust you more during those times. Thank you, Lord, for the lessons learned, but most of all, thank you for your faithfulness to us at all times.

In the name of Jesus, Amen.

Chapter Four

PRAYING AMIDST
THE DARKNESS

*To keep me from becoming conceited because of these surpassingly
great revelations, there was given me a thorn in my flesh, a mes-
senger of Satan, to torment me. Three times I pleaded with the Lord
to take it away from me. But he said to me, "My grace is sufficient
for you, for my power is made perfect in weakness."*

2 CORINTHIANS 12:7-9, NIV

Not everyone's story has a happy ending. There are times
when no matter how much we pray—even praying
together—the answers do not seem to come. At least, not the
answer we want. This was the apostle Paul's experience with
the "thorn in his flesh," and it can also be our experience
when praying together as a couple. We live in a good world
gone bad because of sin. For this reason, there are things that
will happen in our lives that will go counter to what we expect:
We may lose a job, or our life's savings. We may lose a child or
a spouse. No matter how much we pray, the worst that we can
imagine will still occur sometimes.

It can be very difficult to begin praying together when life
is at its darkest. We are broken, paralyzed by the pain, barely
able to function—how do we even begin to pray together

during such times? As we've mentioned earlier, this is one of the best reasons we know for starting to pray together now. When the dark nights come, we want to know how to find each other when we are on our knees before the Lord. We don't want to be alone in prayer during those times.

We don't do this only because we think that we will have more persuasive power before God if we pray together. We do it so that we can stand together with one mind as the dark storm hits us. Yet there are also obviously times when God hears and answers our prayers, but the answer isn't what we want to hear. It's at those times that we need to clearly remind ourselves that the purpose of prayer is not just to "get things," but primarily to build a relationship with God. When we pray with our spouse, our primary objective is to deepen our mutual sense of God and build spiritual intimacy with each other.

Hal and Lee

Hal and Lee Ezell have been good friends of ours for many years. One thing we loved about Hal was that he was always ready to pray with you at any time, about anything. In any situation, Hal might say, "Hey, let me pray with you about that." It didn't matter where you were, he would pray with you there, on the spot. Lee, an author and speaker, tells us what happened when, newly married, she and Hal first tried to pray together:

When I was first married to Hal, we never had a "sweet hour of prayer." We struggled! I always have been the big talker, and, believe it or not, Hal was more on the quiet side. So when it came to praying together, I just took the ball and ran with it. One thought would bleed over into another, as I'd scroll down my prayer concerns. I'd cover every base and then become quiet so that Hal knew it was his turn. But I hadn't left him any room! I'd prayed for everything.

It didn't take long for us to discover the joy of praying conversationally. Just as you would in normal conversation, one of us would introduce a subject—say the children—and then each of us would chime in, leaving our burdens and requests before the Lord about the kids. When we'd covered this topic, we'd go on to another subject—say our friends in Youth With a Mission on mission fields around the world. We'd lay their names and needs before the Lord, back and forth together conversationally. When we were through, we felt so satisfied. I hadn't hogged all the time and run every base; it wasn't a competition. Now it was teamwork, and we were both winning in prayer.

Lee recently lost her husband to cancer. She and Hal had prayed together for many years, and when he was diagnosed with cancer, they continued to pray together. It was a painful time for all of us, but especially for them as they struggled together in the darkness with God over Hal's disease. Lee said,

> I'd be working at the kitchen sink, watching my husband on the patio. We thought the chemotherapy would do the trick—at least that's what the oncologist told us. We were

trusting God for healing, but instead Hal's physical body was wasting away. At the same time, however, I was watching his spirit growing stronger through prayer—especially our prayer times together. He was becoming 'Exhibit A' for 2 Corinthians 4:16, "though outward man perish, yet the inward man is renewed day by day" (KJV).

I especially loved to join him in prayer. Our praying together had changed so drastically since his diagnosis. It went from desperation—begging and pleading—to standing and believing, then to quiet acceptance of the will of God, and resting in his care. We prayed with thanks for the blessing of our children and grandchildren. We prayed with grateful hearts for the precious friends who surrounded us, and supported us with prayer and casseroles! We worshiped the Great Physician, and told him we placed ourselves under his treatment protocol, and our trust was in his plan.

Hal died fourteen weeks after being diagnosed with cancer. But the Spirit of God was preparing Hal's soul for another realm—a realm in which prayer changed into worship and thanksgiving. I should have read the signs and realized my Hal was preparing himself for his heavenly home as I watched him on our patio—he was worshiping Jesus Christ.

At the beginning, Hal and Lee were praying that God would change things—that he would bring the rain. But no rain came. Instead, God changed their hearts and turned the darkness into a different kind of light. That may not be much help or encouragement when someone is still praying that God will change things, but it is an important principle to hold onto. If our only focus in praying together is that we can get something from God, or we can get our spouse to do or be something different, then we are still at the beginning stages of spiritual growth and development. Maturing in our faith means that our focus changes, or, in a sense, broadens. We do not stop asking God for things, but we gradually begin to expand our understanding of prayer so that it becomes more and more a growing relationship with God. We become more involved in the process of knowing God better than in trying to get something we want or need from him.

Gillian and Mel

Gillian Weitsz is a friend we met in South Africa. Her story is similar to Lee's. The rain didn't come for Gillian and her husband, either. She writes in her book, *Riding the Cancer Roller Coaster:*

Losing my beloved husband was the most devastating blow I have ever experienced. We had a wonderful twenty-eight-year marriage. We wondered so many times at how blessed we were. We were at the prime of our lives, children for all intents and purposes off our hands, one of them happily married, and with a lovely granddaughter. A secure future lay ahead of us, as we had planned carefully, spent frugally, and established ourselves in our respective careers. Life had dealt us several blows, but we were blessed with an excellent, loving marriage and were still the best of friends after these twenty-eight years. Above all, we had learned how to pray together and felt that we were developing a deepening spiritual intimacy with each other that was the top-off to a good marriage.

One night while on a holiday my husband complained of a little pain across the diaphragm. We both thought it was just stress and maybe the result of a little overdoing the day before. A few days later a spasmodic cough developed, and it worsened each day. After seeing a local doctor, who prescribed antihistamines and antibiotics, we headed home, thinking he must just need a little rest. That weekend began a downward spiral that neither of us could have imagined would progress so quickly. First an X-ray showed his chest cavity filled with fluid. Next a pleural biopsy was done to determine if tuberculosis or cancer was present. Both my husband, Mel, and I began to hesitantly ask ourselves, "Could it be?"

As we sat and waited for the results of the biopsy, I remember thinking that this happened only to other people, not me, not us. God wouldn't, couldn't be so cruel. We had so much to live for. I tried to pray, but it was mechanical and I felt desperate—*where are you, God?* I identified with David when he said, "My heart is an anguish within me; the terrors of death assail me. Fear and trembling have beset me; horror has overwhelmed me" (Ps 55:4-5, NIV).

The sequence of events from that day on became a blur as I daily tried to cope with the whirlwind of emotions that I felt. I tried to become rational but my heart, and not my head, was in control. The news that there was no hope of recovery—nil, as the doctor said—slowly sank in. Did they realize that they were talking about my husband, the man I loved, a wonderful, gentle, family man with all the qualities I adored—sensitivity, tenderness, and a delightful sense of humor?

We began treatment and the terrible roller coaster of ups and downs that all cancer patients and their families go through. Hope and then despair, hope and then despair. We read everything suggested to us, and hung on to any hopeful thing. We began to hang on to our faith with desperation. We prayed and hoped, now knowing that it was only God himself who gave us the strength and sustenance to get through all that was thrown upon us. We were so thankful that we had learned early in our relationship how to pray together, otherwise I don't know what we would have done. It was our lifeline, our connection, not only with God, but with each other.

God so graciously gave Mel and me some time to laugh and cry together. We discussed death, we discussed my future, we made plans and cried over them. Good days became a joy and bad days a challenge. We read Scripture and prayed aloud, increasing our faith by the minute. I bargained with God and then backed off. We knew that we shared a spiritual closeness and interdependency that few couples experience. We walked the terrible path together, each consoling the other and drawing on reserves of strength we did not know existed. Little things became incredibly important. We were so thankful for our time together.

We never gave up praying without ceasing for healing— knowing so many others were praying for Mel, too. Why hadn't God answered our prayers? My minister suggested that I allow God to decide what type of healing he would give Mel. I slowly began to relinquish to him my anger and my control. I longed for Mel to stay forever, but not as he was then, racked with pain and struggling for every breath.

The end came one sleepless night as I helped him back into bed and knew that the minutes were precious. He died as I held him, with me praying, "Lord, help me release him to your loving arms." What hit me so hard was the finality of death. Where was he? What would I do without him?

Grief is like a disease. It takes a long time to heal. Nobody told me that woven into the pain is also a wonderful gift—the gift of reappraisal of priorities, of renewed faith and discovery of God, of courage yet untapped, of a sharpening of the senses, of an appreciation of the gift of life. In the midst of the agony comes a richness of life and perception that deepens the meaning of existence, giving a greater understanding of "the search for meaning," which Victor Frankl maintains is the purpose of life.[9]

Both of these stories illustrate how praying together strengthened the couple's relationship while circumstances were at their worst. The dark night had come. The answer to their prayers was not what they had literally hoped and prayed for, but God brought them something else instead. Not everyone escapes the darkness—God has never promised that life would be easy. What he has promised is to stand beside us in the midst of the storm, and if we are faithful during that time, we will find that God has brought us a different gift—his presence!

"We're Disappointed With God"

For some couples, even the act of praying together left them disappointed. One husband wrote: "We need help. We are full of anger, bitterness, and fear. Our praying together did not help tame our attacks on each other. When we prayed together we were not able to get answers. We felt empty and unheard."

Another wife wrote: "My current situation with my husband has not improved much for the past five years. We stay married because individually we want to obey the Lord's command-ment—no divorce. But the inside of me has died. Please pray for us."

This wife reported that they had made the commitment to pray together over the six weeks, but were able to pray together only two or three times a week for the first couple of weeks, and that by the end of the six weeks, they had com-pletely stopped praying together. They felt they were unable to penetrate the darkness both of them were experiencing.

Often, disappointment with God in matters of individual prayer, or in what seems to have been God's failure to hear and answer prayer in previous situations, makes it difficult to open ourselves up to praying again. This reluctance to pray is especially strong when it comes to praying with our spouses. The very idea of praying together means we will have to open ourselves more, but we don't want to, out of fear that God again won't hear or answer. If that happens, our disappoint-ment with God will be even deeper.

Personally, we've found it very important for us to remem-ber that the objective of our praying together as a couple is not to "twist God's arm" in order to get what we want. This hasn't been an easy lesson for us to learn, and we are still in the learning process.

DAVE: Several years ago we became involved in a lawsuit which started because the person who bought our house failed to make payments to the bank on a loan he assumed. Over time, the suit became more complicated, but we felt confident that truth would prevail and we would be in the clear. We had a witness from the bank who would back up our side of the story. In addition, friends supported us and gave us promises from Scripture, including the following:

> But in that coming day, no weapon turned against you will succeed. And everyone who tells lies in court will be brought to justice.
>
> ISAIAH 54:17, NLT

And another that says:

> Commit everything you do to the Lord. Trust him, and he will help you. He will make your innocence as clear as the dawn, and the justice of your cause will shine like the noonday sun.
>
> PSALM 37:5-7, NLT

As the trial date approached, we attempted to contact our witness, only to learn that he had recently died. Not only did we lose our case, but we were also directed by the court to make payments on a debt that was no longer ours. We found out that in court, what constitutes truth is defined differently than we had assumed. Where was God? Why hadn't he protected us? These questions raced through our minds, and we verbalized them to God on several occasions. But once again, we had to realize that the purpose of our praying together wasn't just to get what we wanted. Far more important was for us to learn to see things from God's perspective—that he is able to take care of us even when circumstances seem to dictate otherwise.

What we faced again is that the primary purpose of praying together is to build a mutual relationship with each other and with God. It is "keeping company" with God. When we are able to remember that, we find that the literal, specific answer we so much desire may still be our heart's cry, but overshadowing it will be the reality of the intimacy of the relationship, as we together acknowledge God's sovereignty.

Questions to Discuss Together:

1. Read again the passage of Scripture quoted at the beginning of this chapter (2 Cor 12:7-9). Then talk together about why you think God allowed the apostle Paul to have something in his life that was painful.

2. Why do you think God answers some prayers in the positive and some in the negative?

3. When the answers to prayer do not come as we expect them, do you think it is OK to feel disappointed with God?

4. Have you or has anyone close to you lost someone, or have you had a loved one who trusted God for healing but that healing did not come? How did you handle that? How did others around you seem to handle that?

5. How do you think those who lose loved ones are able to see that God is still involved with them and has not turned a deaf ear?

Prayers for Couples to Read and Pray Together:

Dear Heavenly Father:

We don't understand how it is that you allow some of us to suffer pain or loss and don't choose to stop it. How can a God who is loving allow such a thing? Are you going to help us understand this? It seems that this is where the rubber meets the road, so to speak. Why are we to pray together in agreement knowing that sometimes the answer is yes and sometimes it is no? That is really hard to understand. We know that somehow you are way beyond all that, but we need help in sorting it all out. We want to pray and we want to build spiritual intimacy with each other, but we desperately need your perspective on this. We seem to confuse each other when we discuss prayer, especially when we talk about how you answer prayer. It is very difficult for us to find agreement. Give us your wisdom, we pray.

In the name of Jesus, Amen.

⌇

Dear Father in Heaven:

We understand, Lord, but we still don't like it. It seems like you promised to do whatever we ask, if we agree in prayer, yet we know that isn't always the way we experience it. And no explanation really helps us during that time. Lord, we're in one of those times now when we really need you to come through for us. We need your divine "yes!" We don't think we can handle a "no." But as we come into your presence as a couple, we are being honest about the depths of our struggle, and our desire to be dependent on you. Hear the cry of our hearts, Lord, and hear us, comfort us, answer our pleas, and work your miracle. We don't presume to tell you what to do, for you alone are the sovereign God. Help us to rest in you.

In the name of Jesus, Amen.

⌇

~

Dear Father God:

It's always hard to hear "no" as an answer. It was hard when we were children, and it is still hard now that we're adults. It's really hard to hear "no" from anyone, but it seems the hardest "no" is when we hear it from you. It would help if we could hear *why*, but then we know you don't often tell us why. So we know it all boils down to our trusting you. We want to, Lord, but it's hard when we really need a "yes" answer. Help us to learn patience. Most of all, help us to learn to better lean on you and know that in your goodness, even your "no" is because you love us. We want to be a couple that knows you and trusts you. And we realize that the school of "no" can be the best teacher to help us with that. Help us to be good students. We love you and thank you for loving us.

In the name of Jesus, Amen.

~

Part Two

ENCOUNTERING BARRIERS

Chapter Five

SWEATERS AND PEAS

I don't understand myself at all, for I really want to do what is right, but I don't do it. Instead, I do the very thing I hate.

ROMANS 7:15, NLT

JAN: "OK, here's a list," I said to Dave as we were talking about this chapter. "Sweaters, peas, ringing telephones, broccoli, shopping, lumpy mashed potatoes, returning phone calls ..."

"I don't get it."

"OK, here they are again. Sweaters, peas, ringing telephones, broccoli ..."

"Things I hate; things to avoid."

"Close," I said.

"Things I resist."

"You got it!"

"That's not even funny," he said with a smirk. "I guess we are talking about resistance here."

The things our spouses resist are quite evident as we come up against them almost every day. For example, the other day when Dave and I were getting ready to take a short trip to the mountains to lead a couples' retreat, Dave, as usual, went out, got in the car, and actually started the engine while he waited for me to do the last few things I felt were necessary to do before leaving for a couple of days. Needless to say, it would have been more helpful if he had asked me what there was left to do and helped me so that he wouldn't have had to wait in the car, but that is beside the point.

The weather was chilly and I knew that when we got to the mountains it would be even colder. I hurried out, put my things in the car, and climbed into the passenger's seat. As I looked over at Dave, a question somehow slipped out of my mouth before I knew it; "Don't you think you need a sweater or something?" Now, that may sound innocent enough as you read it here, but you have to know that we have a history around that phrase. Dave looked at me with that kind of look that said, "Don't mother me," and replied, *"No, I don't."* My immediate reaction to that tone of voice was to tense up inside, become silent, and feel hurt. Dave, after about ten minutes of silence, said something like, "I guess I just can't be honest with you. You just shut down when I let you know something bothers me, and you know how your silence gets to me."

My reaction, finally, halfway into the trip, was to say, "I was only asking because I care about you." That started the discussion we've had, it seems, hundreds of times. I say, "I may sound like your mother [the mother-in-law I dearly love and respect], but I *am not* your mother and I resent the way you act when I ask just a simple question."

"But you know that I hate it when you ask about sweaters. I never ask you if you need a sweater," was his response. And on and on it goes, as we try to work out our relationship, with its issues revolving around both my resistance and his.

As we talked about it later, we both realized that here was an example of a principle that I have heard Dave teach in counselor training over and over: "Don't look at the obvious. There's always more to it." How many times have I taken personally the responses Dave has given to things I have said that are on the surface a reaction to me? Yet I know that if I stop to take the time, I will see that the things he resists are usually related to earlier experiences that don't relate to me at all. Sometimes they are related to patterns we have set up over the years—things we think we have dealt with and thought we put away. Either way, resistance is not easy to deal with in ourselves or our mates. I have my own list of things I resist, and unraveling the story behind my resistance tells a lot about me, for the what and why of the things we resist always tell a story, one we are not always willing to examine. When it comes to making changes in a relationship—especially a change like starting to pray together—all kinds of things kick in, especially resistance.

Resistance is a complicated concept. The dictionary defines resistance as "the act or power of opposing or withstanding." One of the best ways to understand resistance is to ask a friend to hold up his or her hand. Then you take your hand and begin to push against it. Your friend will almost always automatically begin to push back against your hand, resisting you pushing him or her. When we demonstrate this to a couple, or even to an audience, we will then ask them why they are pushing back, when their only instruction was to hold their hands up. They usually respond with "I don't know," or, "It just seemed natural." That's the nature of resistance—we oppose, or push back, when pushed against.

One of the things we know about resistance is that it is both a natural process and, especially in relationships, an inevitable one. Yet in spite of it being natural and inevitable, we are still usually surprised when we meet it head-on, especially in our spouses. The apostle Paul is baffled by his own behavior in Romans, chapter seven. He knows what he wants to do and what is good to do, but he can't do it. Instead, he finds himself doing the very thing he doesn't want to do. At the end of the chapter he is depressed as a result of resisting the good. The consequences of such resistance are never positive, but we do it anyway. (Of course, we *are* to resist temptation, the devil, and sin, but that is resisting evil, not the good.) Learning how to cope and deal with resistance effectively is one of the basic tasks in life, and it is especially important in building a healthy marriage relationship.

Carol Anderson and Susan Stewart, in their book, *Mastering Resistance,* say,

> Resistance to change in general and resistance to being influenced in particular always occurs when individuals, groups, and systems are required by circumstances to alter their established behaviors. Unless people are immediately persuaded by overwhelming evidence that a change in their behavior is necessary or beneficial, such as responding to a fire by exiting from a building, they will resist change in the status quo.[10]

Even change that is good for us is more often than not the subject of resistance. That's part of the irrational nature of resistance. Why would someone actually resist something that they desire? Why would Dave behave in ways that sabotage something that is good for him, as well as the closeness he wants in his relationship with Jan? Yet what Jan described at the beginning of this chapter is not only irrational, it is a universal experience.

Part of the reason resistance is such a formidable barrier is that it feels so personal. When Dave is resisting the sweater or the peas, it feels to Jan like he is resisting her. Even when Jan tells herself that she's not the issue, it still feels very personal. And when the resistance *is* personalized, the natural response is to either give up—become silent—or to strike back in some way. Either response only perpetuates and solidifies the initial resistance.

That's why when a couple sets out to seek a deeper spiritual intimacy in their relationship, resistance in one or both of the partners usually becomes a barrier to what they actually desire. Unfortunately, some couples find the barrier impossible to overcome.

There's More to Resistance Than Resistance

Part of the reason resistance is so difficult to overcome is that it doesn't just stand alone. Resistance is part of a bigger picture. In a marriage, over time, a common history develops. No one ever really talks about this history—it is just what we have experienced. Within those experiences, we develop behavioral comfort zones. Even though we may say we want to make a change, these zones stay in operation within a limited, specific range.

A perfect example of this limited, comfortable range of behaviors was shown in a short segment on the TV program *Frasier.* In the scene, Martin, the father, and Daphne, a health worker, are preparing breakfast. They go through a whole set of actions that is carefully choreographed. When Martin reaches high in the refrigerator, Daphne is reaching low. Then they switch and it is all perfectly coordinated. When the toast pops out of the toaster, Martin grabs it, says "hot," and drops it on a plate that Daphne suddenly has ready. It is a ritual that we, the viewers, are to assume happens every morning.

Then one thing in the sequence changes. Martin's usual yellow cereal bowl is not available, so Daphne hands him his cereal in a red bowl. He stops and asks why, thus changing the routine, and everything breaks down. They bump into each other at the refrigerator, the toast falls to the floor, and nothing else works. Their comfortable zones of behavior have been changed, and chaos is the result until a yellow bowl is found for Martin's cereal and the balance between their actions is once again in sync.

Now if this were to occur in real life—and it does every day, though not exactly like on the program—the resistance to change would not be a conscious, planned thing. It would be the result of an unconscious reaction to the change, even if it were a desired change. Remember, resistance is a set of behaviors, conscious or unconscious, that interact with other behaviors in such a way as to block change, even if the change is for the good of both people involved.

So what else is in the picture? What we haven't commented on is that whenever change is happening, there is going to be anxiety. This anxiety is over the potential threat to our emotional security that any change, even desired change, is going to create. Our "choreographed" behaviors give us a sense of security—things are predictable. We operate as a couple by unspoken rules that are based on our patterns of behavior. Change something, and our security is threatened.

This was demonstrated by several of the couples who responded to our questionnaire. One couple said,

> When we were able to pray together, we felt not only closer to God, but much closer as a couple. But we weren't very successful. Our intentions were good, and we started out good for about a week but then tapered off. We're praying together maybe one or two times a week, although each of us prays individually daily.

So, even though they prayed individually consistently every day, and even though they had a great experience when they prayed together, they were not able to develop a similar pattern of praying together. They were unable to overcome their unconscious resistance to change. They didn't call it resistance, but what they described is a typical example of resisting change to established patterns of behavior.

Another example is the couple who told us they had a crisis concern within their family. They were able to pray with other people about it, and obviously they prayed individually about it, but they were unable to pray together about it. That may seem irrational, but it too is a classic example of how resistance works. At some level, they each saw praying together as a change in their relationship, and the fear and anxiety that change instilled in each of them overcame the desire to pray together.

Degrees of Resistance

Not every couple will respond to change with the same degree of resistance. The level of resistance in any individual can be seen as being on a continuum that runs from passive on one end to outright rebellion on the other end. It looks something like this:

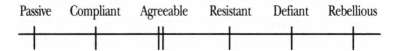

| Passive | Compliant | Agreeable | Resistant | Defiant | Rebellious |

The best place to be is in the range of "agreeable." Here a person will work with the other to create positive changes in their relationship. Every couple has times when things work smoothly and the outcome is positive. One or both may think to themselves afterward, "Wow! That was easy." And so it was. As one moves to the left of agreeable, one becomes "compliant." This may seem positive at first, and at times it may be, but typically, one never knows what is going on inside of the compliant person. Is he just pretending? Is she just being dependent? Does he have any thoughts of his own on this? What is she really thinking?

Compliance may work for awhile, but eventually it will move further to the left, where you encounter passivity. This type of behavior can be very frustrating to a spouse, for now the formerly compliant person takes it a step further and simply says and does nothing. Often the passivity is accompanied by a veiled anger that is expressed in passive-aggressive behavior, which can be very difficult to live with. The passive-aggressive person is sabotaging even those things that are desirable. But this is different from the other side of the continuum and from resistance; the passive-aggressive person who is sabotaging situations will not own up to what he or she is doing. Obviously, the further left one gets from the center—agreeableness—the more frustrating one's behavior and attitudes will be for one's partner.

If we move from agreeable to the right side of the continuum, we will first encounter the resistance we've already described. Over time, the resistant person may become outright defiant, actually saying "no" in the strongest possible terms. It isn't a healthy "no" used to set healthy personal boundaries; it is defiant! Then, further to the right is rebellion, which goes beyond defiance in that it is a *lifestyle* of defiance and resistance. At this stage, the person not only says "no" to the desired good; his or her defiant resistance becomes a way of life in almost every situation. This type of person says no to everything. Often, rebellion is seen as a way to "be myself." In reality, such people are controlled by all the others they are saying "no" to. They long ago gave up their choices in favor of a lifestyle of "no." Obviously, the only healthy spot on the continuum is the space close to "agreeable."

Many factors will influence where couples fall along this continuum. Some resistance, like the example we gave about Dave, will come from their childhood experiences. Some may come from a strong sense of individualism, from earlier patterns in their marriage, or from the level of fear each may have about closeness. It may even come from differing definitions as to what constitutes closeness in a relationship. One person may describe "close" as being open and vulnerable, while another may describe it as a physical thing, like touching and sitting together on the couch.

Sometimes things like moods or events during the day can determine where a couple is on the continuum. A bad day at the office can transform a compliant wife into a resistant wife or an agreeable husband into a defiant one. The passage of time may also move one or both people from being agreeable to either passivity or resistance to any possible changes. We just get more set in our ways. That's why the best possible time for couples to begin praying together is during the engagement period, or at least on the honeymoon. Resistance is typically not in operation at that stage of a relationship, so it is easier to create a behavioral pattern—a comfort zone—about praying together at that point than it may be at a later stage in a marriage. The honeymoon is over when resistance begins.

Overcoming Resistance

DAVE: In looking at my own patterns of resistance, I can see how they correlate with my perception of being controlled. When Jan asks if I have brought a sweater, it just clicks into my mind as "control." Or when she urges me to eat peas (or almost any other vegetable), I know I have said to her, "I'm an adult, I don't have to eat my peas if I don't want to!" That's a control issue for me. In my own personal experience and in my counseling, I've found that resistance is either a response to our fears about change, or perhaps more importantly in my experience, it is a response to my perception of someone wanting to control me in some way. Notice, I said, "my perception." I don't rationally think that Jan is trying to control me when she asks, "Aren't you going to eat your broccoli?" I've learned that sometimes she wants my broccoli if I don't want it. But, as we have just pointed out, resistance isn't rational, so it doesn't respond to facts or logic, and that she might want to eat my broccoli is a fact that is not considered. Even before logic or reason can kick in, I've resisted. It's that quick.

What I've found helps most is for Jan to precede her comment with something like, "Now, I'm not trying to control you, but ..." That may sound silly, or too obvious, but it works for me. Sometimes, but not too often, I can say that to myself: "Now, she's not trying to control you, so relax."

When we are talking about control, we are also talking about responsibility. When Jan is asking me about sweaters or peas, it can feel (notice I said "feel") like she is taking responsibility for something that I am capable of taking care of for myself. That's why mothering always seems to come into the picture. When someone is "mothering" you, it feels like they are usurping responsibilities that you are perfectly capable of handling on your own. Now Jan may not agree that I am capable of knowing if I need a sweater or not, but in my mind, I am able to handle that responsibility. I know that in our relationship, we do best with each other when there is a healthy balance in our interactions, and control and responsibility issues stay in the background. I think that's true with any couple.

If you are encountering resistance in your spouse about praying together, or really about anything else, even sweaters or peas, here's a list of things you can do to make your discussions more agreeable:

1. Check out who it is you really are resisting. You may be resisting your spouse, but the intensity of the resistance may show that it goes far beyond the present discussion. For Dave, it was his mother, always trying to make him eat his vegetables. For others, it might be an abusive parent who hovered over them as they were growing up and punished them for any small infraction. If you can't figure out who it is you are really resisting, talk with your spouse about it—he or she probably knows the answer.

2. Once you've identified who it is you are resisting, talk about examples of what took place in the past that felt so controlling to you as a child. Talk with your spouse about actual situations and try to describe the feelings, especially the fears you had "back then," or may still have as you think about it.

3. As Dave suggested, try to be aware of the old patterns before making suggestions. Then add a phrase like, "I'm not trying to be controlling, I just wondered if ...?" This won't work every time, but it is amazing how a simple phrase like that can defuse a resistant attitude.

4. As you are talking about this, stop and pray about it together. Or have the listening spouse pray for the "remembering" spouse, that God will give them freedom from the patterns of the past.

As we look in the next chapter at some of the specific barriers couples encountered in trying to follow through on their commitment to pray together for six weeks, keep in mind that resistance plays a role in each of the barriers. It's also important to remember that when we encounter resistance in our partners, it is not necessarily a personal issue, even though it may feel like it. Then remember that at the root of resistance is going to be either a fear of change or a confusion of responsibility. Resistance to any change is inevitable, but when you encounter it, put it out on the table and examine its roots, pray about it together, and then move forward.

Questions to Discuss Together:

1. Read together the passage quoted at the beginning of this chapter (Rom 7:15). What do you think the apostle Paul meant when he wrote about knowing the right thing to do, but instead doing the very thing he hated?

2. Why do you think we as humans spend so much of our energy resisting even the good things that are put before us?

3. What role do you think resistance plays in your relationship with each other? What are some of the things you resist? Do you resist any of the things Dave resists?

4. Why do you think it is so hard to make changes, especially changes that affect our marriage relationship for the good?

5. As you look at the different degrees of resistance talked about in this chapter, can you think of examples from your own experience that would illustrate any of the degrees?

6. Where do you think your own resistance comes from? Why do you think it is important to understand where your resistance comes from?

Prayers for Couples to Read and Pray Together:

~

Dear Heavenly Father:

We don't quite understand why each of us puts up such resistance to things that we have discussed with each other that would improve our marriage, especially something as positive as learning to pray together. We are so human and we know that you understand that because you created us! But somewhere there is a need in us to fight against most everything and especially anything that requires some exposure of our soul. Would you give us insight into the past experiences that might be underlying some of our resistance to positive changes? If there are fears that we have not been aware of, will you be there with us as we seek to face them? Help us to begin to listen to each other's fears about change, and give us the courage to talk about them.

In the name of Jesus, Amen.

~

~

Dear Father in Heaven:

We are really thinking about how difficult it has been for us to make significant changes in our lives. We are beginning to understand that so much of our resistance to change is because we are afraid of the unknown. We are pretty comfortable in our way of life and frankly, it scares us to open ourselves to you in deeper ways because there's always the chance you might ask us to face something really hard. Things are going well and it just seems like we want to leave well enough alone. But we know that in your Word, Jesus teaches that our lives are to be paradoxical—we are to give up our lives in order to gain them. Help us to understand how that works. We really want to risk going deeper with you and with each other, but we need you to work in us to increase our faith. We want to trust you for the strength to get through any tough times that may come. Will you give us the courage to do this?

We ask this in the name of Jesus, Amen.

~

Dear Father God:

At least one of us doesn't even like to consider the fact that we are resistive. Maybe it's both of us. We do it, but we don't like to admit it, even to ourselves. So, Lord, we are admitting it to you, and ask that you help us to better understand ourselves. Give us the courage to look at the roots of our resistances. Give us the freedom to be able to talk with each other about those roots, helping each other dig out the roots so we can find the freedom to act in ways we really want to act. Give us patience for the journey as well, Lord, and walk beside us in the process. We are so grateful for your presence in our marriage, and ask that we will sense, to an even greater measure, your presence alongside us in these difficult areas of our lives. Thank you for your faithfulness, and for loving us as we are.

In the name of Jesus, Amen.

Chapter Six

WE WANT TO, BUT ...

But Jonah got up and went in the opposite direction in order to get away from the Lord.

JONAH 1:3, NLT

I t's difficult to get away from the Lord. Jonah found that out the hard way. Yet even though we have the examples in Scripture of those like Jonah who took the hard way and we know the consequences, we still resist what we know to be good. It would be hard to say whether Jonah was more rebellious than resistive, but the consequences remain the same. He was swallowed by a great fish. For us, the consequence is that we lose any sense of intimacy. We may not go so far in our resistance as to actually run away from our spouse or from what the Lord wants; yet we still find ways to make it impossible to do what we really want to do.

Resistance takes many forms. Some couples who volunteered to pray together wrote back to tell us they were unable to follow through on their commitment. They weren't being openly rebellious; they were, however, resisting something they had wanted in their lives. And they were willing to tell us why. They described some of the obstacles they experienced in trying to pray together. Others, who were partially successful, who either prayed together for a short part of the time or prayed only one or two times a week over the six weeks, were able to identify the obstacles they faced as well. Here are the main barriers they identified.

"Our Lives Are Just Too Busy"

The most common problem couples experienced had to do with busyness, or, as they often put it, "time constraints." One couple referred to it as the "tyranny of the urgent." A wife and mother wrote: "With three kids ages six and under, it was extremely hard to find a time when my husband and I could pray together without falling asleep."

They had made a commitment to pray together every day for six weeks, and she added that it had taken them seven weeks to get started, and for three weeks they had been successful. Once they started, she said that it was much easier to pray together than they had expected. Perhaps their fears about praying together were as big an obstacle as the time constraints. But then the pressures of family took over and they were so distracted that they forgot about praying together.

Others reported that they were so overwhelmed by circumstances that even though they wanted to pray together, and knew it would be good to pray together, they didn't. One wife said, "I know praying together every day would be extremely beneficial—especially in our current circumstances. We pray a lot with others, but rarely just the two of us. I don't know why, except to say that we're tired and mostly overwhelmed these days."

One couple said that on the days they had family devotions together at dinner, they didn't want to take the time later to pray together as a couple. They just weren't as motivated. It was as if they had already fulfilled that need, so now the pressures of family all too easily overrode their commitment to pray together. Busyness is one of the more common ways many of us resist change.

"We Like Doing Things Different Ways"

Some couples' individual personalities with the accompanying styles and expectations get in the way of praying together. You could even say their differences sabotage their efforts.

For example, let's say you like to pray individually at the same time every day, perhaps early in the morning. In fact, one could set the clock by watching your routine. You like structure and schedule, and that's how you want to handle praying together. Your spouse, however, has a different style. (It's amazing how often a structured person ends up marrying someone who is open-ended and loves spontaneity.) He or she may like to pray while exercising, while driving to work, or even in the shower. There's no set time, just the reality of praying regularly.

It's easy to imagine the struggle that will take place when you try to set a time to pray together. After some frustrating attempts at getting started, you may both back away from the task completely, because your spouse simply doesn't want to "do what makes sense." You may stop talking about it. Or, if you do talk, the guilt each of you feels may cause you to blame one another, even though the real problem is your differing styles.

When styles differ, compromise is a must. Choosing to do things either one way or the other, with no accommodation for differing styles, would be wrong. Somewhere in the middle lies the solution. Of course, neither person may be totally happy with a compromise solution, but at least the couple will have a solution to the problem, and as they implement it, they will find that it works. Compromise is a way of recognizing each other's needs, and the only thing that *will* work over time.

"We Have Different Sleep Patterns"

Different sleep patterns and work schedules were another problem couples identified. One partner liked to go to bed early and the other liked to stay up late. Of course, the opposite was true in the morning. It was hard for these couples to find a time when they could pray together. One wife, who was a night person, simply told her husband to wake her up early for prayer, and she would go back to sleep afterward. Her husband wrote a little note to us next to her comment, saying, "We'll see how long she'll last." He had to leave for work at 5:40 A.M.!

Several couples solved their problem of differing sleep patterns that same way. One husband who left early for work had permission to wake up his wife so that they could pray together, and they'd been doing this successfully for more than a year. Another couple solved this problem a bit differently, by having the wife, who was a night person, stop what she was doing and pray with her husband before he went to bed. We often do this when Jan is busy at night and knows she's going to come to bed late. She'll stop what she's doing and come to pray with Dave.

"We're Just Plain Lazy"

A number of couples said they had to overcome their own "laziness." They actually used that word! It's true—it takes effort to pray together regularly. These couples were very honest about their struggle. A number found that by making a commitment in writing to us, they worked harder at finding the time and overcoming the inertia of old behavior patterns. Perhaps what they called "laziness" was simply the ease of being caught up in comfortable patterns.

In addition to the "laziness" obstacle, others said that they often simply forgot. In some ways, each depended on the other to remind them, and then no one did the reminding. Having made the commitment, however, these couples did eventually come back to it and start praying together again.

"I Don't Feel Safe With My Partner"

Several couples said that they were afraid of praying together, especially praying out loud. One wife said she was afraid of having anyone, especially her husband, even hear her pray. She added: "Prayer is so personal. It was scary to open up in the one area in my life where I feel most vulnerable. I felt like I was letting my mate see me at my most vulnerable, naked moments."

We have already quoted the wife who said that at first she didn't feel safe praying with her husband, because after she told God her needs, her husband would try to fix them. After she talked to him about it, he was much more careful about trying to help God answer her prayers.

DAVE: I think the issue of safety was also a big problem for me, not because Jan was unsafe, but more because I had my own difficulties with trust and letting someone get that close to me. It was easy to blame all kinds of other things, but down deep I believe I was afraid to be known by Jan at this level of intimacy. At the time, I would have strongly denied such a thing. After all, I was a man. I could not admit to being afraid. Yet there was no other way to really explain my holding back.

One couple to whom Dave referred earlier described praying together as "being spiritually naked together." We've talked about the special kind of vulnerability in praying together that requires the mutual ability to trust. In a marriage relationship, unless something has happened to destroy our trust of our spouse, our ability to trust him or her is usually not an issue that is based on the qualities found in the other person. It is first of all based on an issue within ourselves. That was certainly true for me. Trust was easy for me as long as closeness wasn't involved. There is nothing I can see in Jan that would lead me not to trust her in anything. She wasn't the issue. In the same way, I could trust friends, though it was more difficult to trust close friends. If the problem had been based solely on the trustworthiness of other people in my life, the opposite would have been true. It would have been easier to trust those closest to me. The problem was within me.

My ability to trust was shaped by my early experiences within my family. I came from a very detached family. I didn't know that growing up, for I thought my family experience was the norm—I had nothing else with which to compare it. So when I would say my family was close, that was my experience, but I began to realize that, compared to other families, my family was not close, especially emotionally.

When I got married, I thought I wanted more emotional closeness than I had experienced in my family. Yet I found that when I was asked or expected to do anything that might lead to emotional and spiritual closeness, an alarm would go off within me, and I would find a way to back away from what, at another level, I truly believed I wanted. I was resisting the very thing I wanted. Finally, as I described earlier, I had to "bite the bullet" and face my fears. I had to stop listening to the internal alarm and move into areas that felt very unsafe and scary to me. When I did that, I started to learn about trusting and about the intimacy I truly wanted.

"We Have Too Much Conflict in Our Marriage"

There were a variety of ways that couples dealt with conflict and praying together. One couple said they took a "strife break" from praying for a day. Most couples said that when there was conflict within the marriage, they didn't pray together that day, but by the next day they were either "over it" or had talked it through and they were able to pray together again.

One couple said that they tried to pray together when they had a fight, but they admitted that, at least in the beginning, they were trying to "preach" to their partner through their prayers. Obviously, this didn't work, and they then realized that they were simply masking their fight by calling it prayer. This "preachy prayer" forced them to talk about what had been troubling them.

One wife wrote about her reluctance to pray with her husband due to a conflict, then described how God had prompted her to resist the natural temptation to ignore praying together:

> Just this morning, when it was time for my husband and me to pray together, I struggled with it. A seed of bitterness toward him had started to sprout, and after a restless night of sleep, I had thorns of anger ready to rip at his flesh. I could feel myself start to spiral out of control, and God wisely prompted me to say, "Ken, let's pray."
>
> I poured my heart out to God, sharing my anguish with Ken through God's filter of prayer. This snipped the rough edges of "self" and allowed Ken to respond kindly to my frustration.
>
> When we rose from our knees, I was a new woman. I smiled and hugged my husband, silently thanking God. Only the Lord and I knew how different the day could have turned out if we had not prayed.

Another couple said that they simply hadn't even tried to pray when they had had a fight, but later they found that both of them had trouble sleeping. That motivated them to try harder to work things through before going to bed. Most of the couples reported that their prayer time brought them to a point of discussion and resolution, either before they prayed or soon after.

JAN: Often, when we are having problems we maintain our prayer time together, but it's not easy. By the time we are to pray together at bedtime we usually are not speaking. That night, one of us, usually I, will break the silence and say, "Are you going to pray?" Dave will usually answer "No," to which I will typically reply, "Well, I'm going to anyway." Often, by the time I'm done, Dave will be ready to pray. Then, when we have finished praying, we will work through the source of our conflict. Obviously, there have also been a few times when neither one of us was willing to pray, and when that has happened, we haven't worked through the issue until the next day. Over the years, though, we've found our prayer time to be a great source of accountability in our marriage. Our commitment to praying together overrides our desire to avoid the issues between us.

One couple who told us they kept their commitment to pray together even when they had a conflict, said they did so simply out of obedience to what they believed God wanted them to do. As they prayed together, however, they would each talk to God about their part of the conflict, often even taking responsibility for what they had or hadn't done that had led to the problem, and then asking God for his forgiveness. They were careful not to preach at the other. This has led them to some very tender times together, and to a greater sense of intimacy.

It's very difficult to be that honest, even before the Lord, when everything inside wants to defend your side of the argument. Obviously, when we are at odds with our spouses, our first task is to repair that relationship. Then our prayers will be heard and we will be able to hear each other's hearts once again.

Overcoming Barriers to Prayer

Each of these problems, in some way, relates to a basic, underlying fear we all have—that of being known at the deepest levels of our being. So we resist. Praying together, among other things, exposes the level of intimacy we are already experiencing. If I say, "Let's pray together about this," I am demonstrating the degree of comfort and ease I feel in the relationship. But if I become uncomfortable when my partner suggests to me that we pray together, I am revealing to myself and to my spouse that I am not at ease with some part of our relationship. If I can avoid praying with my partner, through busyness, laziness, time schedule differences, or even personality differences, I can avoid whatever discomfort I am feeling about our relationship.

Many things in the world can press in on us and keep us from praying together. We know this well from our own personal prayer experiences. We each live hectic, pressured lives and have much sympathy for those who confront these barriers. When you add the pressures of two lives together, it is easy to see how the spirit can be willing, yet the flesh just won't cooperate. Over and over again, couples have reported to us that the commitment they made to us in writing to pray together every day was a major factor in both their ability to get started and their ability to continue.

Making the commitment definite is the beginning. Then one of the best ways to overcome barriers to shared prayer is to talk together about the priorities in your marriage. It's interesting that while we set goals and objectives for our work, our retirement, our kids, and our ministry, we often think that marriage, and in particular a spiritual marriage, will just happen if we each do the right things. We've found in our marriage that nothing happens without a plan and without our having stated our dreams and objectives.

We went away one weekend some years ago to the mountains. Our purpose for the weekend was to discuss what we wanted for our marriage. We worked out a "mission statement" for our marriage. We came up with this purpose: To be facilitators of healing in relationships. Then we talked about our goals as a couple. How did we want our kids to remember us? What message did we want our friends to hear from us about our relationship? What were our priorities going to be, apart from the kids and our family responsibilities? That weekend was a very important time for us, for a lot of pieces fell into place about our priorities for our life together. Our only wish was that we had done it years before, at the beginning of our marriage.

Since you've read this far, it is clear that you want to experience spiritual intimacy in your marriage. Why not stop reading and see if you can start a conversation with your spouse about the goals and objectives of your marriage, especially in regard to the spiritual?

Questions to Discuss Together:

1. Look up and read together the story of Jonah in the Old Testament book of Jonah. (It's short—only four chapters.) Discuss what you see in the story that suggests Jonah is being resistant to what God wants from him.

2. Earlier in your marriage, what has kept you from doing the things you felt you needed to do? In what ways do you think these obstacles or barriers are a form of resistance? What are some of the obstacles you are facing in your desire for spiritual intimacy in your marriage?

3. Some of the obstacles described in the chapter are really just a result of who we are, like sleep patterns and personality differences. How can resistance become a part of these natural differences?

4. Have you ever tried to pray together during or after a conflict? What happened? Have you ever thought about praying together then, but didn't say anything? Do you remember why you didn't say anything?

Prayers for Couples to Read and Pray Together:

Dear Heavenly Father:

We don't like the idea that our busyness is really a form of resistance. We really are busy; too busy! But what do we stop doing? We have kids to take care of, parents to worry about. Our finances are always close to the edge and we can't cut back on our working. And the few times we have tried to pray together at the end of the day, we've found we were just too tired and fell asleep. We don't think it's resistance; it's just the way our life is today. But please show us where we are using our schedule to avoid what we want. We do want to find spiritual intimacy as a couple, but how do we add even one more thing to our schedule? There's no room, not if we are to remain sane. Help us, God. Help us understand what you want from us. Help us sort out what is really important, and if there is something we can let go of, help us see how. You know our hearts—we don't want to resist spiritual intimacy. You know we long for it together. Help us see how we can begin.

In the name of Jesus, Amen.

Dear Father in Heaven:

Making prayer a top priority sounds so easy. But how? With our schedule, we've tried and failed too many times. We feel too discouraged to try again. So where do we begin? What do we change? We both know that when we've tried in the past, it did make a difference. Why did we stop? Help us understand, Lord. We talk about making changes in our schedule. We know we seem to talk about it all the time and never do anything to change it. We need help. At this point, we even need your help when we try to talk about praying together. Show us what can be different. Give us the courage to stick with it this time. We know you can help us, so please do so. Start with showing us where to begin. We thank you in advance for your help.

In the name of Jesus, Amen.

~

Dear Father God:

We're grateful, Lord, that we've been able to pray together, but we long to do so more consistently. We thank you that you've helped us get started. Now we need your help for the long haul as we seek to become more consistent in praying together every day. It seems that the joy and intimacy we are experiencing should be enough, but life is hectic and other people and responsibilities press in on all sides. Help us to stay vigilant so we can be prepared for the pressures when they come. Help us to stay focused so we can learn better how to shut out the unnecessary things that come into our lives. Give us the courage to help each other stay focused on you.

In the name of Jesus, Amen.

~

Chapter Seven

FACING THE UNSEEN

Be careful! Watch out for attacks from the Devil, your great enemy.
He prowls around like a roaring lion, looking for some victim to
devour. Take a firm stand against him, and be strong in your faith.
Remember that your Christian brothers and sisters all over the world
are going through the same kind of suffering you are.

1 PETER 5:8-9, NLT

There are unseen forces of evil that want nothing more than to keep you and your spouse from praying together. Couples who pray faithfully soon know that they are in a battle with those forces. Since there is such power when two agree in prayer, the enemy seeks all kinds of reasons to keep us from praying together. One couple said it this way:

Praying together, for us, has been worth the effort. I've been told it takes three weeks to make a habit, but it is so easy to blow it away. Every once in awhile, Satan will throw all sorts of things at us. But we've found that if we hold tight to our commitment, even when we miss a few nights, we get right back on our knees ASAP.

Obviously, praying together doesn't prevent the enemy from hurling his darts at us. In fact, as we begin to pray together, we will quickly find that we are engaged in a battle against a formidable enemy. Bad things happen in our lives. The question is, how are we going to handle these events? God has a plan, and Paul gives us that plan. He lays it out for us, describing in Ephesians 6 the weapons we have for doing battle with Satan. Surrounding his description of those weapons, he says,

> Be strong with the Lord's mighty power. Put on all of God's armor so that you will be able to stand firm against all strategies and tricks of the Devil. For we are not fighting against people made of flesh and blood, but against the evil rulers and authorities of the unseen world, against those mighty powers of darkness who rule this world, and against wicked spirits in the heavenly realms.
>
> Use every piece of God's armor to resist the enemy in the time of evil, so that after the battle you will still be standing firm....
>
> Pray at all times and on every occasion in the power of the Holy Spirit. Stay alert and be persistent in your prayers for all Christians everywhere.
>
> EPHESIANS 6:10-13,18, NLT

To pray is to enter into a spiritual battle. As Jack Hayford has said, "prayer is invading the impossible."[11] It is our basic weapon in the fight against the evil one. Therefore, one of the best ways to thwart the enemy is to make praying together a regular practice right from the beginning of your relationship.

Of course, that's not possible for many of us who didn't start at the beginning, but here are some examples of what can happen when couples do start praying together right from the start.

Kathy and Mike

Kathy Deering has been our editor for this book. As we talked together about our subject, we discovered that she and her husband Mike have prayed together ever since the beginning of their marriage. They were willing to share their story:

> We were new Christians when we were married, and we decided to start praying together on our wedding night. We established a pattern of praying together just before going off to sleep and have not missed a night in twenty-eight years. When one of us is away from home, we pray separately before going to sleep, knowing that the other person is doing the same thing.
>
> On the few occasions when one of us has been too sick to pray, the healthy one has prayed for both. We usually go to bed at the same time, but even when we don't, the one who is first to retire seeks out the night owl spouse for a moment of prayer together.
>
> Our prayers are simple: Usually Mike prays first for me—for my night's sleep, for anything that needs special attention, and for the next day. We call it "praying for daily bread," as in the Lord's Prayer ("Give us our daily bread")—provision for the next twenty-four hours. We

don't like to project our prayers too far into the future. The day's own trouble is usually sufficient prayer material!

Then I pray for Mike along the same lines. The thrust of the prayers changes as circumstances dictate. Often one or both of us insert special prayers for one of our four children, or for friends who have urgent needs. Our children, now ages fifteen to twenty-one, know that they are prayed for on a regular basis.

After I pray for him, Mike, as the head of the family, usually ends our time together with a prayer for the safety of our home during the night, taking authority over the evil one. As the children grow older, he more often prays for their safe return late at night, for their protection if they are on trips or living elsewhere, and for their decisions. In general, the tone of the prayers is, "Lord, keep our feet on the path of righteousness and our hands in yours."

Once, a few years ago, I wondered whether perhaps our prayers had become too routine to be effective. So often we used the same phrases. So often we were incoherent with fatigue. Sometimes, especially when all four children were small, I would ask my husband, "Did we finish praying?" because I had fallen half-asleep as he prayed. It just seemed kind of flat, so I asked God to show me if we needed to do something different, like maybe pray sitting up (we usually prayed lying in bed side by side). When I asked God this question, I heard his loving rebuke immediately and clearly in my mind: "YOU HAVE NO IDEA HOW IMPORTANT YOUR PRAYERS ARE!" God's voice was so startling and clear that I reported it to Mike, and we have never since questioned the value of our prayers.

Because we pray together daily about simple matters, we have found that when bigger troubles strike, we are well equipped to pray together. We have prayed our way through life-threatening illnesses, the severe mental illness of a family member, seven years of infertility, three miscarriages, sudden unemployment, financial trials, major decisions, the deaths of parents and friends, and the teenage rebellion of one of our children.

We have found that our prayers are painfully hindered when we are at odds with each other—in fact, it is impossible for us to pray until our contention is cleared up. We feel we enjoy one of the healthiest, happiest marriages around, and it's a chicken-and-egg question as to whether our prayer life has enhanced our communication or our communication has enhanced our prayer life. All we know is that it flows together very, very well, and that one could not proceed effectively without the other.

Mike and Kathy set a pattern early, and have been careful over the years to heed the apostle Paul's warning to "pray at all times." They have seen God at work in so many areas of their lives, and who knows how many spiritual battles have been won because of their faithfulness?

Jim and Karen

Another couple, Jim and Karen Kingma, attended one of our seminars in Michigan. They have been praying together since before they were married and know the power that prayer has brought into their lives. Recently they started a prayer ministry in their church. Jim described some of what he's experienced through their communal prayer:

There is *nothing* that can take the place of falling on our knees together to cry out to our Father and share our deepest needs in prayer with him. The spiritual intimacy that has resulted has been amazing. We have laughed together, cried together, and rejoiced with each other in prayer. It has brought a sense of oneness that is really indescribable. In our relationship, our praying together has deepened our love for each other.

One of the important things I've learned over the years is that God is who he says he is. Even during those times when it felt like God was late, or when it seemed like there was no answer to our prayer, looking back we can see that he has always been there and has never been late—his timing is always right. I know for me that as we pray together—and we started when we were dating—I can fear no evil and I know that God is directing my life's path.

We have discovered that quite often we have both received a prayer burden for someone specific. We haven't talked about it, but when we both pray for that person, we are amazed at how God has laid that burden on both of our hearts. Later, we've often found out that the person we prayed for really needed prayer at that particular time. I don't know why we're so amazed at what God does, but we still are. It's exciting to be part of God's battle with the evil one in our world today.

Karen added her thoughts:

I have learned that praying together really knits us to-gether as a couple. It hasn't been easy. Jim gets up at 4:30 A.M. and I get up around 8:00 A.M. And of course, Jim goes to bed long before I'm ready. But we worked it out from the beginning that whenever one of us goes to bed, that's the time we pray.

Over the years, I've learned that Jim is very tender to the Lord, and he truly desires to be the spiritual leader in our home and a man of integrity. Because we have become so vulnerable in our praying together, it helps me trust Jim even more. We have prayed about everything—from lust to what kind of car to buy. It has all brought us closer to each other and to the Lord. One of the interesting things is that I believe I can really trust Jim because I know his spiritual temperature by his prayers.

In Ephesians 4:26 Paul gives us another warning about the unseen forces around us. He says, "And don't sin by letting anger gain control over you. Don't let the sun go down while you are still angry, for anger gives a mighty foothold to the Devil." In earlier chapters we've heard from some couples about how they have handled conflict—here's what Jim said:

We have our conflicts just like any couple. What we try to do first is talk things through. Then we are careful to ask for each other's forgiveness, regardless of who was at fault. Finally, we get on our knees together and ask God for for-giveness. We then ask him to help us in these difficult areas of our life to live victoriously, for we know it is part of the enemy's attack on us as a couple. God has been so faithful in helping us. It is wonderful, after having an argument, to give it to the Lord—it works for us!

When faced with a crisis, it is easy to forget that a spiritual battle is raging around us. We are too much like Elisha's servant, who could see only the material reality. To him, all was hopeless. He and Elisha were both "goners," he thought.

But Elisha could see beyond the obvious reality to the spiritual reality. His perspective changed everything. When Elisha asked God to allow his servant to see beyond the material, he was able to see "that the hillside around Elisha was filled with horses and chariots of fire" (2 Kgs 6:17). Prayer opened his eyes, and prayer opens our eyes to what God is doing, for it is then that we enter into his reality.

James Houston, in his book, *The Transforming Power of Prayer,* has said, "Encountering darkness in our lives should not drive us from prayer, but drive us to prayer. Darkness only becomes an obstacle when we fail to see God as the powerful ruler of our lives, able to overcome the evil we face in spite of our own fears and feelings."[12]

It's important to be able to pray together in a crisis. But it is even more important—and more powerful—to be able to pray together daily. Only in this way can we guarantee that we will provide no foothold for the enemy.

Several years ago we spoke to a large group on this subject. A pastor was in the audience. Months later he invited us to come and speak on the same topic—couples praying together—at his church. As we were waiting for the program to begin, he said to us, "My wife and I have been married for forty years, and we've been in the ministry for almost that long. We've always been able to pray together when there was a crisis, but we never developed the practice of praying together daily. A year ago, when we heard you speak, the Lord challenged us, and since then we have not missed a day of praying together. We can't begin to tell you the difference it has made in our lives and in our marriage."

As we talked together, he tried to describe the difference, and the only thing he could come up with was, "It's like a peacefulness has come over us." Perhaps they were like Elisha's servant—now, they are not only aware of the evil one in the world, they are more aware of God's activity in the world, and in particular, in their own world. The forces of evil are there, but the "horses and chariots of fire" belonging to the Lord are also there!

Questions to Discuss Together:

1. Read together again the passage quoted at the beginning of the chapter (1 Pt 5:8-9). What does this passage say to us about priorities?
2. What are the priorities in your marriage? Discuss them and then together write them down.
3. If you've started praying together, have you noticed that anything has gotten worse? If so, discuss together how this can be part of doing battle spiritually.
4. Do you ever think about the invisible spiritual forces that are all around us? Have you ever had any experience

similar to Elisha's servant, perhaps not in actually seeing God's invisible army, but in knowing that in some way God was fighting alongside you as you faced the enemy? Talk about this idea with your spouse.

5. In what ways can you see that praying together is part of your "spiritual armor" for your marriage?

Prayers for Couples to Read and Pray Together:

~

Dear Heavenly Father:

It does feel like we're in a battle and it also feels like we're losing. We try to use the armor Paul talks about, but it still feels like we're weak and powerless. We've tried standing still so that the battle can be the Lord's. We've tried praying and reading the Bible, but we just can't see how these are weapons. The battle going on in our lives just seems too overpowering. Where are you in this battle, God? Can you teach us how to use the weapons of Scripture and prayer better? We're like Elisha's servant—all we can see is the enemy. We don't know where you are, God. Please show us your power. Help us become better fighters in the spiritual war going on inside us and all around us.

We ask this in the name of Jesus, Amen.

~

Dear Father in Heaven:

We know the battle is spiritual and we know that prayer is essential. We feel the attacks of the enemy of our souls, not only on us personally, but also on our marriage. We pray for victory, Lord. We want to see your hand of victory in our lives. But we feel defeated in spite of what we know and believe. Help our unbelief and our doubts. Protect us by your mighty hand. Surround us with your angels. Fight the enemy on our behalf, O Lord. We want to trust you. We want to be victorious. Please fill our marriage and our lives with your power and your presence.

We pray this in the name of Jesus, Amen.

~

Dear Father God:

You are the mighty one. The battle is yours. Your forces have already defeated the enemy. We claim your victory in our lives and in our marriage. [List some areas in your marriage and family where you claim God's victory.] Help us, Lord, to ever be mindful that we are in the midst of a spiritual battle that you have already won. Help us, as we face the unseen in our lives together, to have the eyes of Elisha, who was calm in the face of the storm, because he could see your power—he could see the unseen. Give us that kind of vision in our lives, we pray, O Lord. Thank you.

In the name of Jesus we pray, Amen.

~

Part Three

BEGINNING THE JOURNEY

~

Chapter Eight

STEPPING OFF THE CURB

My house will be called a house of prayer for all nations.

ISAIAH 56:7, NIV

S everal years ago, we were listening to a series of messages given by Ron Kline, then head of the missionary radio ministry of HCJB in Quito, Ecuador. He had organized his messages around the idea of a great parade that spanned the centuries. He started by naming some of the great saints in Scripture—sort of his version of Hebrews 11. He talked about Peter and continued with the apostle Paul. He then led us forward through time, touching on the great men and women of faith through the ages. He finished by naming and describing some of the unknown saints of today that he had met around the world—incredible men and women in Eastern Europe, in Russia, and in other remote parts of the world. These were people who, in spite of the opposition, were examples of great faith.

He painted a marvelous word picture for us, suggesting that all of these people were marching by in a parade in front of us, celebrating and participating in the things God has been and is doing in the world. He then pointed out that we each have a choice. We can stand there on the curb and watch the parade go by, cheering each as they pass us. We can even get excited and tell other people to come and watch the parade. We can watch for awhile, yawn, and then go home and forget about the parade. Or we can step off the curb and join the parade! We can join God in what he is doing in the world today. We can become participants, and the choice is ours.

As couples, it's hard to make that first step off the curb. But we challenge you to just jump in somewhere and join in what God wants to do in this world through you as a praying couple. Here's how to get started.

Getting Started

Here are eight suggestions for beginning to pray that were given to us by the couples who responded to our questionnaire. They come from their own experiences and were developed through their own struggles to begin to pray together.

1. Take the time needed to talk with each other about your thoughts and feelings about prayer and praying together. Do this without pressuring one another or trying to make the other feel guilty. See if you can agree that this is something you both want in your marriage. Talk about your fears in as open a way as possible. Talk also about your expectations up front, so they don't undermine you later on.

2. Pick a specific time and make a commitment to each other to begin praying together at that time. You'll never get started praying together on a regular basis if you don't make this definite commitment to a specific, agreed-upon time.

3. Don't be upset if you miss a day. It's important, if you miss a day, to just start again the next day. Consistency will come over time. Let yourself off the hook here.

4. Decide who will do what. For example, who decides where you will pray together? Who reminds the other that it is time to pray together? Couples reported that they couldn't just make a commitment to a time and then assume both of them would remember. It helped for one person to take on the responsibility to say, "Hey, it's time for us to pray together." It was interesting to note that for the couples who were successful, it was more often the husband who did the reminding.

5. Start where you are both comfortable. This means that if only one of you is comfortable praying out loud, then you don't start there, for both aren't comfortable at that place. If one of you insists that you pray together silently, then both can be comfortable at that place and that's where you begin.

6. Set a time limit. It was surprising how many couples made this point. "No long-winded prayers," they said. One wife wrote, "No long monologues with fourteen items in them!" Another couple suggested, "First start small and grow from there. Anyone can pattern five or ten minutes into their lives, as opposed to one hour." Another couple said, "Start with five minutes and then gradually, over time, see what

happens. Don't try to take too much time as you begin."

7. Agree at the beginning that neither one of you will preach in your praying. Nothing can stop the process like using the time to pray together as a way to preach to your spouse, or to make suggestions in your prayer. Sometimes just making this a rule will give a reluctant spouse the freedom to get started, for a common fear is that one's spouse will use this time to preach rather than to pray.

8. One husband suggested: "Start with a list of things you want to pray about. This could be done individually or together. Then pray individually about your time of praying together before you actually come together for prayer."

How Do We Pray Together?

Now that we have the plan, what do we do as a couple when we pray together? A basic premise to keep in mind is the importance of praying *for* each other. Although the Bible doesn't say directly, "Husbands and wives, pray for each other," it does say in James 5:16 (NIV, TLB) that we are to "pray for each other so that you may be healed." That certainly includes husbands praying for wives and wives praying for husbands. One couple said, "Every time we pray together, we begin by praying a blessing over each other. We do this to edify our spouse and make them feel loved."

One of the things we do is find different prayers in the Bible and then agree to pray them for each other. For example, one of our favorites is a prayer Paul prayed for the Philippians in chapter 1, verses 9 and 10 (NIV). He writes,

This is my prayer; that your love may abound more and more in knowledge and depth of insight, so that you may be able to discern what is best and may be pure and blameless until the day of Christ.

We've found this prayer to be a beautiful expression of what we want to experience in our marriage. We often use it as our theme verse for the couples' retreats we lead. Here's the way Dave would pray this for Jan:

Father, I pray this for Jan, that her love will abound more and more in both knowledge and depth of insight, so that she will be able to discern what is the best, and will be pure and blameless until the day Christ returns.

You might want to read through Paul's letters, and other books of the Bible, looking for prayers that you can pray for each other. This can be a very meaningful way to pray for your spouse. If you don't use these prayers when you actually pray with your spouse, then show your spouse the passage and explain that you are saying that prayer for him or her.

Now that you are praying for each other, here are six ways you and your spouse can pray together. Regardless of your experience or comfort zones in praying together, there is one way of praying together that anyone can experience.[13] (This is the first method listed below.) If you are already praying together, look to see if there are any additional ways you can enjoy praying together with your spouse.

1. Pray silently together. All too often, couples believe that they are praying together only if they are praying out loud. Remember that the key is to intentionally pray together. When we are talking about this with couples' groups, we suggest that they begin by praying silently. Here are the guidelines: First, sit down together and hold hands. A number of couples have commented on how important it was to be touching each other as they prayed together. Next, talk together about some of your mutual concerns as a couple. Then, as you finish the conversation, one of you should say to the other, "Let's pray about these things." Finally, spend some time in silent prayer together. Whoever finishes first should squeeze his or her partner's hand as a way of saying, "I've finished." When the other person finishes, he or she squeezes back. Congratulations! You've just prayed together.

   After doing this for a time, you might say "Amen" out loud as you finish and squeeze your partner's hand, and then wait for him or her to say "Amen."

2. Finish silent prayer aloud. The second way you can pray together is an extension of the way we have just described. It takes us a step further in becoming more open and more comfortable praying together. Instead of simply ending your silent prayer with a verbal "Amen," agree that after a squeeze of the hand, the other person will finish their silent prayer out loud. This does not have to be profound. Simply say something that expresses thanksgiving and praise for the knowledge that God is present with you and that he not only hears your prayers but also knows and hears the deeper needs of your hearts. Or thank God for

being present with you, in both your time of conversation and your time of prayer.

3. Write out your prayer. First, write out a short, simple prayer that is meaningful to you. Do this apart from your partner. Then come together and read your prayer to your partner. After you both have finished, you may want to discuss your positive responses to each other's prayers, and how it felt for you to hear one another talk to God. Or read together some of the prayers we have included at the end of each chapter.

4. Pray as you talk. This approach to praying together simply means we back up in our conversation and consciously include God in the process. As a couple, you can simply stop in the middle of your conversation and suggest, "Let's pray a moment about this." If you're at the silent stage of praying together, pray silently about what you've just been talking about.

If you are verbalizing your prayers, you can simply acknowledge that God is a part of your conversation. For example, when we are talking about a concern we have, one of us might simply say, "Lord, you are here listening as we talk, and we want to acknowledge your presence and ask for your help with this situation." Even this can be simplified, or the other person may add a sentence or two in prayer. We seldom say "Amen" when we do this—we just go back to our conversation. Over time, God's place within your conversation will become more natural, and you will become more aware of his presence.

5. Pray out loud, together, daily. This is the same as our earlier suggestions, except that you are now comfortable

enough with the process that you can verbalize your prayer in the presence of your spouse. In our questionnaire, we asked couples to tell us how they moved from praying silently together to praying out loud (meaning, was it difficult?). We wanted to know if couples talked about it beforehand, or if it just happened. We were surprised when a number of them such as the couple we mentioned earlier, replied, "We opened our mouth and said ..." We laughed, but it really does boil down to that approach—opening our mouths and saying out loud what we are praying inside.

Over the years, as we've become more comfortable with verbalizing our prayers together, we have expanded our evening prayer time to other times of the day. When we are together, one of us may feel the need to pray, so we stop and pray. It is more just a part of our conversation, even though we are still purposely stopping to pray together.

6. Practice "vulnerable" prayer. This type of praying together is what we think most husbands (and some wives) fear is what we have in mind when we talk about praying together. It is difficult, and we certainly don't suggest starting this way. In vulnerable prayer, we pray about ourselves in the presence of our spouse. Along with praying "Lord, help us," or "Lord, help them," we pray "Lord, help me." When we pray this way, we are comfortable enough with each other that we can bring forward, with candor and honesty, our weaknesses, our failures, and our struggles, and talk openly with God in the presence of our spouse.

This type of praying together is listed last, not because it is the best, but because it is the most difficult. Some couples may never pray this way, while others become very comfortable praying this way and feel that it is this type of praying together that really enhances their spiritual intimacy. Remember, however, the goal is not to pray vulnerably together; it is simply to pray together, consistently.

What Do We Pray About?

There was a consensus on what different couples prayed for. The most common response was to pray for their immediate family. Couples prayed for their children, both young and old. They prayed for their parents and for their siblings. Many prayed for themselves in relationship to their family— for example, a husband praying to be a better father to his kids. The health and safety of family members was a very important prayer concern. Couples who had been married before often prayed for resolution of past hurts with estranged family members.

As a part of praying for family, many couples noted that they prayed for their own relationship. Often their prayer related to their marriage was an expression of praise. Others talked about praying for the difficulties in their marriage and how God answered their prayers. Many noted that they also prayed for their physical relationship. Couples reported specific answers.

Probably the next most common theme was the prayer for direction in important decisions. Couples prayed about buying or selling a house, and about job changes. Others faced major difficulties in their businesses or jobs, and prayed for guidance.

Many noted that they prayed for their pastors and their church. Also, many prayed for missionary groups, or individual missionaries. Others who were in ministry often prayed for those to whom they had ministered in the past, or those to whom they would be ministering in the future.

Also important were the needs of friends. Many prayed together for the salvation of friends and family members. Some prayed specifically for other couples they knew who were experiencing marital problems. They prayed for their own boldness in bearing witness to others about their faith. Several noted that they had prayed for an opening with a specific person so that they could share their faith, and God had answered in some amazing ways. Some prayed that a friend, or a family member, would find a spouse. They called it spiritual matchmaking.

Finances were a big topic in many couples' prayers. A number noted that God had carried them through a financial crisis during the time they had committed to us that they would pray together. Some couples also prayed regularly for those less fortunate than they. They prayed for the poor and needy in their community. They prayed for the advance of God's work in the world today.

Nothing was beyond the prayer concerns of the couples with whom we talked. In addition to all of the above requests and issues, most commented on the fact that part of the time spent praying together was devoted to worship and praise, not just for what God was doing in their lives, but simply for who and what God was in their lives and in their marriages.

Does God Get Bored?

Kathy Deering earlier alluded to this question, and it is one we have discussed in our own experience. After all, when you pray almost every day, it is easy to fall into a routine and not say much that is different each time. We sometimes get bored with our own prayers, so why shouldn't God?

But he doesn't! Perhaps it takes being a grandparent to really understand this. We have noticed that we never become bored with our grandchildren. They come over often, since they live close by. While we speak with them frequently, the kids, especially the younger ones, don't really have much of a range of subjects for conversation. They read the same books over and over again. The truth is, however, they could sit and talk with us about the same things every time they came over and we wouldn't be bored. We love them too much. All we need to do is reflect for a few moments on how our love for our grandchildren has left us no room for being bored with them, and we know the answer to our question about God.

We often sit and just marvel at the uniqueness of each of our grandchildren. When we were parents, we had moments like that, but we were too busy being parents to spend much time at it. It's much easier as a grandparent. We see the changes in them each time they come over. We listen carefully to everything they have to say to us. We can do that now, for we aren't busy trying to parent them—we just enjoy them. Perhaps grandparenting is more like the way God relates to us, since it's hard to picture him as a harried parent. We may get bored with ourselves, but he loves us even more than we love our grandchildren, so there's no way he could get bored with us. It's pretty incredible to think that when we come into the heavenly Father's presence, he simply enjoys our being there with him.

There was one other important focus in a number of couples' prayers. They were praying for real miracles to take place in their relationship. They prayed for healing for the past. There's more about this topic in the next chapter.

Questions to Discuss Together:

1. Consider the verse quoted at the beginning of the chapter (Is 56:7). Can you make the commitment that your house, and your marriage, will be characterized by prayer?
2. What does it mean to you to "step off the curb" as a couple?
3. Perhaps you've already started. What helped you get started praying together?
4. What do you think it means to "pray a blessing over your spouse"? How have you done it? If you haven't, pray a blessing over each other the next time you pray together.
5. Have you felt as you were praying, either as a couple or as an individual, that God was bored with your prayers? How have you handled that issue?

Prayers for Couples to Read and Pray Together:

Dear Heavenly Father:

As we've been reading these prayers together, Lord, we realize we've begun the process of praying together. Thank you, Father, that we can come into your presence and that you welcome us. Thank you that we've started praying together. As we continue in this journey together, we look forward to the spiritual intimacy we will share with each other and with you. There are so many things we can pray about together as we, in a sense, "walk in the cool of the day" with you. Help us to remember that you are never bored with us, and that you always are pleased when you see us come to visit you. Thank you for your love and care in our lives and in the lives of our families. We give you praise for who you are.

In the name of Jesus, Amen.

Dear Father in Heaven:

What a joy it is to realize that you welcome us into your presence. We can come boldly before you, the creator of the universe, because you love us, you have adopted us as your children, and you have invited us to sit and talk with you. Thank you that we can come as a couple, and that you value highly our marriage relationship. We want to be a couple that brings honor and glory to your name, and we realize that we are better equipped for that task because we have together spent time with you. Thank you for this privilege.

We pray this in Jesus' name, Amen.

Dear Father God:

We love you, Father God. We are thrilled that you love us and that you seek to bless us as a couple. Thank you that our marriage is important to you. When we consider how majestic and awesome you are, we are humbled by the fact that you care for us. You love us. You enjoy us. You even enjoy our interactions as a couple. Help us to remember that in everything we do together as a couple, from our arguments to our physical intimacy, you enjoy us and every facet of our relationship. We are your creation, and you are pleased with us, especially when we invite you to be a part of who we are and what we do together. Bless us and our marriage with your presence in every way.

We pray in Jesus' name, Amen.

Chapter Nine

THE HEALING POWER OF PRAYER

Confess your sins to each other and pray for each other so that you may be healed.

JAMES 5:16, NLT

Several couples have talked about the healing power they have experienced in their marriage by praying together. This healing has sometimes been physical, but more often it has been relational.

It's hard to imagine a couple that is barely hanging together actually being willing to pray together. It's hard enough for the couples who are doing well with each other. Yet we've already made reference to Dave's asking couples who are in counseling to begin praying together, especially when they have had a heavy conversation about the troubles in their marriage. We both know of his healing in our own relationship.

One couple who made the six-week commitment to pray together told us that at the time they made that commitment, their marriage was almost over. They both agreed to the commitment as a last-ditch effort to save their marriage. Did the praying together make a difference? Here's what Sam, the husband, wrote:

Praying together strengthened our marriage. We were in trouble before we did this. We really had a marriage in name only. But we put on a good front for everyone else and only those close to us really knew how troubled our marriage was. When we attended your workshop, we both said, "Why not?" when you asked for couples to commit to praying together. I don't think either of us thought much about what we were doing.

You can understand that we didn't begin the next day. In fact, it wasn't until we got your questionnaire about eight weeks later that we actually started praying together. Over the past three months, we've prayed together at least four days a week, and some weeks every day.

Now we've made it a regular routine in our marriage. For me, it's often the only time I get to find out what's on my wife's mind on a given day. Since we're both morning people, I've just made it a practice to set the alarm a little earlier (we get up at 5:10 A.M. now instead of 5:30 A.M.), so I guess I've taken more responsibility for making sure we pray together. But if we miss a day, we don't get upset or disappointed. We just start again the next day or the next.

We understand each other better now and we've gained a lot more respect for each other. We know things about each other's hearts that we wouldn't know if we didn't pray together. I've found for me that it sets my mind in a godly pattern at the beginning of the day and I'm able to handle stress through the day much better. We've also found that we are somewhat comfortably accountable to each other. It just feels good.

His wife, Jeri, was a little more direct about the state of their marriage when they started praying together. She wrote:

Praying together was a last resort for our dying (dead!) marriage. We had so much that was negative in our marriage. We fought a lot about our kids. I don't think we agreed on much of anything. But the real issue for me was that I felt I hardly knew Sam anymore. It seemed all that mattered to him was his work.

I couldn't tell you anything major that happened week to week as a result of our prayer time. But all of a sudden there was a buildup of healing evident, and in hindsight, I can see that day by day, week by week, month by month, progress has been made every step of the way even though I didn't realize it as we went along.

One thing I am aware of is that our praying together has given me a sort of window into my husband's heart. When we were on vacation, we didn't pray together in the morning (though we did continue with our family devotions at dinner), and I started to feel a real lack of connectedness with Sam—similar to what I had been feeling before.

I've found that when we pray together, I definitely feel closer to Sam. As a result, I've been able to let some old hurts heal because I see his dedication to our prayer. It makes me feel so good that I am that important to my husband that he would do this with me!

Some of the answers to our prayers have included our healed marriage and much more unity in raising our children. One specific answer involved my feeling that Sam was not open to the seriousness of our daughter's relationship with a young man. I slowly began praying for this daughter and her future with this man. After some time, Sam began praying for them as well. Through this, God prepared Sam's heart for the time when our daughter's boyfriend came to ask for my husband's blessing and permission to marry our daughter.

I truly believe that the Lord has honored our commitment and follow-through to pray together regularly by blessing us with a marriage that is now very much alive and loving.

Sam and Jeri's story is an exciting example of the healing power of prayer, and especially of praying together. At one point Sam and Jeri described how they held hands when they prayed together. Jeri explained that when they had had a disagreement, they still prayed together, but "the hand-holding was like two dead fish flopped on top of each other."

Still, their commitment to pray together forced them to be together. Jeri said that through their praying together, she "definitely felt more connected to Sam. I finally knew what was on his mind and how to pray for him throughout the day." That alone added to her feelings of satisfaction within the marriage.

A couple we were working with in Dave's counseling office had come because the husband had had a brief emotional involvement with another woman some five years earlier. His wife hadn't known of it, but about a year before, he had begun to feel intensely guilty about what he had done, and had felt that he needed to tell his wife. He was totally surprised by her reaction. What he didn't realize was that he had

had five years to try to resolve his feelings about what he had done, but it was totally new and fresh to his wife, and she was hurt and angry.

In fact, she was so hurt and angry that for the next year their marriage was basically one conflict after another. Finally they came for counseling as a last chance to hold their marriage together and to seek healing for the past. They came about the same time we were asking couples to commit to praying together for six weeks. Dave decided to challenge this couple the same way.

As a part of their counseling process, Dave asked them to limit their conversations about the husband's emotional affair. They were to talk about it only at a certain time each day—a time they chose. Then the conversation was to be limited to no more than thirty minutes. At the end of the thirty minutes, they were to stop and pray together for each other.

At first, they didn't want to do this, for it seemed that talking about it was exactly what they had been doing for the past year. Still, they hadn't been praying together, so they agreed to the plan. Over the next three to four weeks, there was a gradual softening within the wife. When Dave commented on it, she agreed and said the main thing that was helping her was being able to listen to her husband's heart as he prayed about the things they had been discussing. She said, "His sorrow over what he did is far more intense than I knew, and so is his desire for the Lord. I'm beginning to believe he really wants changes in our relationship, and his vulnerability before the Lord has helped me begin to trust him more." They were definitely experiencing healing for their past as a result of praying together.

The Power of Forgiveness

One of the things that happened with Sam and Jeri, and is happening with the other couple, is a process of forgiving. We've found in many situations that praying together destroys the root of bitterness and allows a spirit of forgiveness to grow. Many people walk around with a feeling inside that their spouse "owes them" in some way. There is a payment due for some past hurt. As long as they have that attitude, forgiveness is far away. A biblical definition of forgiveness is "canceling a debt."[14] When I forgive, the other person no longer owes me. I have canceled the debt. What makes it so hard for couples to forgive each other? We have identified five reasons.

First, we find it hard to forgive because we think that we have to forgive quickly, that it is somehow more spiritually mature to forgive quickly. We look at verses like 1 John 1:9 (NLT), which says that "if we confess our sins, he [God] is faithful and just to forgive us." That forgiveness is instantaneous. I don't have to wait and see if God will forgive or not— I know immediately that he has forgiven what I've confessed.

What we forget is that we are living in the period of time following the cross. If we had lived three thousand years ago, about the time of King David, and we had sinned, our forgiveness wouldn't be instantaneous. There would be a long process involved, in that one would have to confess to a priest; offer a sin offering; wait for the Day of Atonement, when the priest would take the sins of the people and offer a sacrifice; sprinkle the blood on the mercy seat; and then put one's sin on a scapegoat, who would be led out of the camp and into the wilderness. This was an act of faith based on something

Jesus would finalize on the cross a thousand years into the future.

So, if we look at the whole span of history, God's forgiveness hasn't always been so quick. There were thousands of years when he took his time forgiving, waiting for the appropriate moment, when, on the cross, forgiveness would be completed. Part of the reason he took his time was because he wanted us to know that sin is serious. If God could take his time forgiving, why are we in such a rush?

Now if something minor happens to us that we need to forgive, we need to forgive it right away. But there are some hurts that are deep and painful, and it may take some time for us to work through our feelings to a point where we can make a conscious act of forgiving. If we rush to forgive, it minimizes the offense.

Second, I think people find it hard to forgive because they can't forget. We've been amazed at how many people still act on the belief that if they forgive, then they must forget. Conversely, if they haven't forgotten, then they haven't forgiven. Once again, we want to be God-like in our forgiving. We know that when God forgives, he forgets. We want to do the same. What we lose track of is that when God forgives, he has nothing to learn in the process, for he knows everything. When we forgive, many times we need to remember, for we often need to learn some things in order to protect ourselves or those we love. Our memories really have nothing to do with whether or not we have forgiven. God forgives and forgets; we forgive and need to remember.

Often the hurts that we are in the process of forgiving, or the hurts we have been forgiven of are painful and we don't want to remember. This is especially true of things that happen between marriage partners. Things are done to us by our spouses, things that hurt deeply, and over time, as we forgive, we wish we could forget, but we don't. In many of these situations, we probably shouldn't forget, as we need to learn something about ourselves and our mates. The solution is that when we remember the pain, it is important that we also remember the forgiveness, and that seems to put it into the right perspective.

Third, we often hesitate to forgive because we think that forgiving will somehow condone the wrong that was done. Here our faith can help us, for we know that when God forgives sin, he never makes sin OK. It is still evil; it is just forgiven. We need to remind ourselves that our forgiveness is not for the benefit of the other person, it is for our own benefit. Forgiveness brings us freedom from the burdens and hurts of the past. It never makes the evil OK, it just frees us.

Think about it for a moment. If you harbor a grudge or resentment toward someone—say someone at church—what happens when you see that person walking toward you? Usually you head off in another direction. You avoid that person. Now, who is controlling your life at that point? You? Or the other person? Obviously, he or she is in control of your behavior. When you forgive that person, you are freed. You won't need to head the other way, for the problem is now that person's alone.

Fourth, we often don't forgive because we forget how much we've been forgiven. Several times, Jesus coupled our being forgiven with our being able to forgive (see Mt 6:9-15; 18:21-35.) The point of the story of the unforgiving servant is that he cannot forgive his fellow servant a small debt because he has never fully realized that the king has forgiven him an impossible debt. If he had internalized the scope of the king's forgiveness, he would have easily forgiven his friend the small debt.

When I am having trouble forgiving, especially forgiving my spouse, I need to remind myself again of how much God in Christ has forgiven me. He canceled a debt of sin that I owed that I could never repay. In that context, there is nothing that can occur in my life or in my marriage that is beyond forgiveness!

Fifth, and finally, we sometimes don't forgive because we confuse forgiveness with reconciliation. They are really two separate processes. I can forgive and never be reconciled, for forgiveness is something I do individually. I don't need your participation in the process for me to forgive you. Although that may make it easier, it isn't necessary. We see this with God. He didn't need our help in the task of forgiveness—that was accomplished by God alone on the cross.

On the other hand, reconciliation requires that both parties be involved in the process. In a marriage, this means that true reconciliation requires both parties to be involved—it's never an individual issue, like forgiveness.

In most relationships other than marriage, reconciliation is optional. In a marriage, when a deep hurt has occurred, reconciliation is always our objective. But both parties must be involved in order for reconciliation to occur—two hearts that are open. This may take some time, but that's OK. Healing always takes time.

By praying together, we have the best foundation, not only for forgiving, but also for reconciliation. The healing power of prayer is best experienced as we come *together* with our hurts and disappointments before the Lord and allow him to do his healing work in our relationship.

Other Types of Healing

We have had couples describe to us other acts of healing as well. Several described a physical healing that they experienced after their partner prayed for them about a physical problem. In another situation, a wife explained how, over the years, they had struggled with her husband's emotional problems. She described for us how praying together had made a difference in her husband:

As a couple we have been praying together off and on for many years. Before we started to pray together, I was very concerned about the fact that my husband would not only cut me off, but also cut himself off from whatever he was feeling. He basically hid from any kind of emotion. He has always struggled with depression. His thinking was very negative and his actions toward me were less than encouraging.

I think it was out of my concern for him that I suggested we pray together regularly. It's been a number of years now since we first started, and we've been pretty consistent over the years.

In the time we have been praying together, I have seen a real, though gradual, transformation in my husband. It seems like God has been strengthening his mind. His burdens, which used to overwhelm him, no longer do so. Now he seeks in prayer to give the troubles over to God, and he has increasingly been able not only to do that, but also to leave the trouble with God. His heart is also much more tender toward me. He doesn't run from his emotions any more, and that's a real dramatic change for him.

Not everyone will experience such dramatic changes. Not every couple needs these types of healings. Still, God is faithful to provide what each of us needs, especially when we are faithful in meeting together in prayer with him.

Questions to Discuss Together:

1. Read again the verse quoted at the beginning of the chapter (Jas 5:16). Do you think this applies to couples confessing to each other and praying for each other?

2. In this chapter, we are talking more about the vulnerable type of praying. Why do you think this is so difficult for couples to do?

3. What are some things that have happened in your marriage that have been difficult to talk about? What do you think would happen if you talked about them, and then finished the conversation by praying together?

4. What are some of the myths about forgiveness that you have believed true at some time?

5. Discuss any situations where you have either personally experienced some type of healing, or know someone who

has, through prayer and forgiveness. Do you think it was related to the principle in James 5:16?

Prayers for Couples to Read and Pray Together:

~

Dear Heavenly Father:

We need some healing in our marriage, Lord. Part of why we have started praying together is the hope that somehow, you will intervene in some way and bring about a freshness, maybe even bring about life again in our marriage. We look good on the outside, but inside, Lord, we are at the end of our ropes. Neither one of us wants it to continue like this. We ask your help. We ask for your healing. Bring life where there is deadness. Bring joy where there is pain. Bring hope again where there is only despair. Come, Lord Jesus, and renew our marriage.

In the name of Jesus we pray, Amen.

~

~

Dear Father in Heaven:

How wonderful it is to read of couples who have experienced your healing in their marriage. We are grateful, Lord, that we are on relatively stable ground in our marriage, but there are areas where we need your healing touch. Help us to confess to each other our needs in these areas, so that as we confess and pray for each other, we release your healing power within us. Thank you for new life together and we look forward to your continuing touch in those weak areas within us.

In Jesus' name, Amen.

~

~

Dear Father God:

Thank you for the healings we have experienced in our marriage. Thank you for being active with us, pulling us, pushing us, walking beside us, and always being there ready to heal the brokenness we have experienced. Truly you are the God of new beginnings. You are a healing, loving God. And we thank you for what you have done in our marriage and for what you will continue to do, as we stay open to you and to each other. Give us courage for the journey ahead and the perseverance to stay focused. Give us patience with you and with each other, and help each of us to have honesty and integrity within as we seek to walk more closely with you. Thank you, Lord, for all that you are, all that you will always be, and for who you are in our marriage. We give you praise.

In Jesus' name, Amen.

~

Chapter Ten

A TIME FOR COMMITMENT

God is love, and all who live in love live in God, and God lives in them. And as we live in God, our love grows more perfect.

1 JOHN 4:16, NLT

Prayer is an essential part of "living in God." Therefore, as we reflect on John's words, we realize that God has promised to those couples who seek to live in closer communion with him that their love will grow more perfect, that is, "whole" or "complete." What a promise!

James Houston comments on everyone's need to have what he calls "prayer companions."[15] He is advocating the necessity for all believers to cultivate personal accountability through prayer with another person. In his discussion, he suggests that that companion be one's spouse.

He goes on to say that "in such times of soul friendship, it is of first importance to understand the threads of each other's emotional history within the family, and how it has affected our attitudes toward God." We agree completely. There is no relationship in which it is more important to mutually understand emotional history and its effect on the relationship not only with each other but also with God, than the one between husband and wife. A prayer partnership with a friend is a wonderful gift between two people united with the purpose of deepening their relationship with God. Jan has had a prayer partner, a close friend with whom she has been meeting weekly for prayer, for more than fifteen years. She and her friend share and pray for the needs of their families and friends, and talk and pray about their own relationships with God. How important this is to her! But the prayer time between us as husband and wife takes on a different emphasis. We not only pray for our family and its needs, we together ask the Lord to use us as a couple in more meaningful ways in his kingdom and seek more intensely to hear each other's heart. Both relationships are important, each with a different focus.

So what are you going to do? Are you ready for the commitment? While you decide, here are some more stories of the many couples who have "stepped off the curb" and started praying together daily. A husband wrote:

> We always experience a sense of peace and contentment when we pray together, knowing the Lord is able to take care of the concerns that are too big for us to handle. As we grow in this area I appreciate more and more the gift of a spiritually discerning wife. Our praying together creates an intimacy that makes us closer in all other areas of our marriage. It is well worth the time invested.

A wife wrote:

> When we pray out loud together, we feel not only closer to God but to each other. By sharing what's on our hearts and minds, we usually find out so much more about our

spouse's worries, frustrations, and so on. This is truly our best form of communication, not only with God, but also with each other.

Another couple wrote:

It starts our day off in the right direction. It brings us closer together. It also brings us peace when we're dealing with difficult issues because we know we are both committed to hearing from the Lord rather than pushing our own individual agendas. We know what concerns each of us because it is voiced in our prayer time.

A husband wrote:

It seemed like when we committed to pray together, more troubles came our way, and as a couple we had to deal with them all. But because we were praying together, we remained intact and we looked to God to resolve the difficulties.

His wife added:

We found that the more we put God first, as it says in Matthew 6:33, the better our overall lives were. The pain and the struggle didn't go away, but it wasn't the nagging, persistent type of pain. We just knew it was there, but we also knew that God was there and he was giving us strength and peace.

Another husband shared:

I believe God intended a couple to work together in raising their family. Spending time in prayer together allows me to gain insight into how my wife is thinking and feeling. As a result I can better "support her with prayer, and encourage her to develop God's gifts to her." (That's a quote from our marriage vows of twenty-one years ago.)

What About You?

Are you ready to make the commitment? If so, fill out the commitment form at the end of this chapter. (You don't need to tear it out—in fact, just fill it out and keep it in the book.) Then write to us and let us know that you've made a commitment to pray together on a daily basis for six weeks, or let us know if you are already praying together. As we have said earlier, there is something about putting it in writing that makes it more definite and real. We will commit to pray for you as you pray together. You can write to us at the following address:

Drs. Dave and Jan Stoop
1151 Dove Street, #150
Newport Beach, CA 92660

Or E-mail us at:
djstoop@deltanet.com

Or you can even fax us at:
949-250-9193

In return, we'll put you on our mailing list and keep you posted on what's happening with other couples who pray together.

OUR
COMMITMENT

B*eginning on* _____, 20__, *we commit to begin developing the discipline of praying together as a couple. We agree to pray together on a daily basis, as much as is possible, for a period of six weeks.*

Name _____

Date _____

Name _____

Date _____

Notes

1. Dallas Willard, *The Spirit of the Disciplines: Understanding How God Changes Lives* (New York: Harper and Row, 1988), 156.
2. Richard Foster, *Prayer: Finding the Heart's True Home* (San Francisco: HarperCollins, 1992), 7.
3. Marriage Ministries International, P.O. Box 1040, Littleton, Colorado 80160.
4. William Barclay, *The Gospel of Matthew, Vol. 2* (Edinburgh: Saint Andrew, 1957), 210.
5. Barclay, 211.
6. Quin Sherrer, *How to Pray for Your Family and Friends* (Ann Arbor, Mich.: Servant, 1990), 143.
7. See Paul Stevens, *Marriage Spirituality* (Downers Grove, Ill.: InterVarsity, 1989), 42. He notes a number of these writers and their reservations about bringing spiritual disciplines into the marriage relationship.
8. Quoted by Barclay, 211.
9. Adapted with permission from Gillian Weitsz, *Riding the Cancer Roller Coaster* (Pretoria, South Africa: Engedi, 1995).
10. Carol Anderson and Susan Stewart, *Mastering Resistance* (New York: Guilford Press, 1983), 1.
11. Jack W. Hayford, *Prayer Is Invading the Impossible* (New York: Ballantine, 1977).
12. James Houston, *The Transforming Power of Prayer* (Colorado Springs, Colo.: NavPress, 1996), 51.
13. These are adapted from David Stoop, *Seeking God Together* (Carol Stream, Ill.: Tyndale, 1996), 57ff.

14. For an expanded discussion on forgiveness, see David Stoop and Jim Masteller, *Forgiving Our Parents, Forgiving Ourselves* (Ann Arbor, Mich.: Servant, 1992).
15. Houston, 310.